The Life, History and Magic of
THE HORSE

warfare were quickly emulated throughout all of Christian Europe. In the lands it had helped to conquer, the Arabian horse long outlived the faith of the men whom its ancestors had borne from Mecca and Damascus. First to eastern Europe, then to western Europe, Islam brought its magnificent horses. But nearly a thousand years would pass before a name, Byerley Turk, would be given to the first of the three stallions to come from this region and begin the annals recorded in the British stud book.

We know that the combination of natural selection in the wild and man's growing comprehension of selective breeding was hardly peculiar to the desert lands of Arabia. The understanding was common to all civilized areas of Europe, Asia, and Africa. What was unique to the horse breeders of Islam was the development of an animal that joined speed with endurance to such a marked degree. Not until the accident of Justin Morgan's celebrated stallion in the late eighteenth century would so comprehensively endowed an animal be discovered. The great horse of northern European climates could carry a much heavier burden than the Arab and for longer periods of time, but not so rapidly. The Barbs, the Turkomans (Turkmenes), the Syrians, and the horses of Turkistan had singular virtues that have been absorbed by the hundreds of distinct breeds which they have sired.

Master and Horse

During times of war, and especially through stallions and mares that were among the spoils of victories, the horses of all the peoples of Europe gradually intermingled and evolved into breeds useful for different purposes. But for

ABOVE: TWO SPLENDIDLY MUSCLED STALLIONS PREPARE TO CHALLENGE EACH OTHER FOR DOMINATION OF A HERD IN THIS JAPANESE DRAWING OF THE HEIAN PERIOD (794–1185). (KOZAN-JI, KYOTO)

OPPOSITE: IN THIS ILLUSTRATION FROM A 15TH-CENTURY INDIAN MANUSCRIPT, THE STORY'S PROTAGONIST EXERCISES HIS HANDSOMELY ORNAMENTED HORSE. (FREER GALLERY OF ART, WASHINGTON, D. C.)

given Guinness' stout as a reward for a fine performance. Inexplicable temperament has resulted in a continuing bewilderment about man's real relationship to the horse. The creature has remained one he has been able to dominate only by separate and patient exercises of wit and will—and yet it is a creature on which he was once utterly dependent, especially for success in the ritual of war.

Whatever the explanation, man continued until the end of the long medieval period to regard the horse with a bizarre mixture of contempt and awe. The horse was a paradox. While obediently carrying man or pulling his vehicles, the animal retained a quality of independence and dignity that was rather godlike. He rarely responded like a dog, for instance, to a peremptory command; he had to be coaxed, wooed, flattered, as wise old Xenophon had advised centuries before. But because man could ultimately compel the horse to submit to his demands, he was simultaneously inclined to despise and abuse the animal —for the very reason that, once broken,

many centuries, man remained puzzled by certain of the animal's idiosyncrasies that had to be taken seriously. These are particularly remarkable in matters of behavior and dietary preference. Some horses, for example, are inclined to shy, to buck, or to tear away unpredictably. A French trotting champion evinced a desire to eat only artichokes. Arkle, the great Irish steeplechaser, was

the horse became so subservient. Thus did man harbor two contradictory views of the creature.

Without the horse, humans would have been immeasurably less capable of becoming significant factors in the world they inhabited. The horse, along with the ship, placed in man's eager grasp the possibility of empire. The distinction between these two means of conveyance was critical. The horse was animate; he could thus be brutalized. But the ship, while of man's devising, was always at the mercies of the winds and seas, quite beyond any sort of human control except prayer. No one, however, broke a bottle of champagne over the head of a mare as she was on the point of foaling, and intoned, "God bless this horse and all who ride on him."

Medieval Mythology

There are a few gods vaguely configured like the horse. However, in most cultures that have left us written or graphic testaments to their beliefs, horselike creatures have been, instead, agents of the gods, and agents of man as well.

In medieval times, the unicorn was as familiar a figure as the centaur had been during the age of the Greeks. He is of unknown origin. Some theorists suggest that the legend was inspired by the rhinoceros, another creature of the *equidae* strain. The Greek historian and quack, Ctesias, described a beast whose conformation was like that of a young horse except for a pointed, spiraling horn protruding from the middle of his forehead, the length of the horn being as great as a yard. Aristotle parroted this description, echoing the assertion that the animal was indigenous to India. The unicorn was, necessarily, foreign to all who mentioned him; every passage about this creature in literature alludes to an animal seen or depicted by someone else—or, if beheld by the writer, seen while he was either dreaming or drunk.

The unicorn was always endowed with powerful magic. To drink from a cup made from a unicorn's horn was to ward off poison, a conviction that lasted until the Reformation period in Britain and until the revolution of 1789 in France. It is worth noting that the uni-

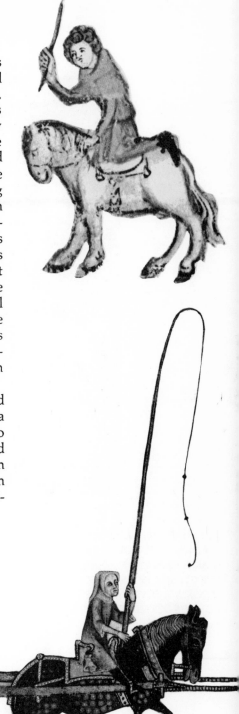

corn was not invariably horselike. Some important images show him as a bovine, as in the celebrated Unicorn tapestries.

The range of imaginative representations of the horse in icons, sculpture, and painting is limitless. But all, however exotic, imbue the horse with god-like qualities. This holds true even in the New World, where the horse did not reappear until the sixteenth century. When the horse returned to South America with the *conquistadores*, the natives lost little time in attributing miraculous powers to him. "El Morzillo," a horse in the little company of Cortes, had been lamed and left behind to perish when the Spaniards departed from the area of Central America that is now Guatemala. The creature which had carried the dreadful Spanish words of God, gold, and European cruelty in the New World became a symbol of terrible natural calamities.

The literature of the early Middle Ages abounds with improbable references to one prodigious horse or another. Apart from the Norse, Icelandic, and Celtic tales, there is the earliest of the *chansons de geste*, in which the accounts of the Chevalier Renaud is one good example. His redoubtable steed, Bayard, bore the knight and three of his brothers in their flight from the wrath of the emperor Charlemagne.

Where do we get the notion of the horseshoe as a symbol of good fortune? Since the object itself is of comparatively recent origin, so too must be the superstition associated with it. One of the earliest and most attractive tales comes from the apocryphal career of Saint Dunstan, the tenth-century Archbishop of Canterbury. In addition to his virtues as Primate of all England and spiritual advisor to the Wessex kings, he is said to have been a scribe of exquisite talent, an accomplished musician and chorister, a bell founder, and a smith. Naturally, it is to the last-named attribute that we owe the legend of the miraculous horseshoe:

Late one night, while Dunstan was amusing himself at his forge, the cloven-hoofed Satan appeared at his door and demanded that the farrier-cleric repair one of his shoes. Dunstan, being a good Christian and therefore a charitable fellow, readily agreed. But once he had the

LEFT: A POPULAR SAINTLY THEME, IN WHICH THE HORSE PLAYS A MAJOR PART, IS DEPICTED IN SAINT MARTIN AND THE BEGGAR, FROM THE BOOK OF HOURS OF CATHERINE OF CLEVES. (THE PIERPONT MORGAN LIBRARY)
ABOVE: ANOTHER VERSION OF SAINT MARTIN AND THE BEGGAR COMES FROM THE LIVES OF THE SAINTS. (FITZWILLIAM MUSEUM, CAMBRIDGE UNIVERSITY)

SAINT GEORGE AND THE DRAGON IS
PROBABLY THE MOST POPULAR OF SAINTLY
THEMES INVOLVING THE HORSE. THE THREE
INTERPRETATIONS SHOWN HERE ARE, LEFT TO
RIGHT, AN ILLUMINATION FROM THE BOOK
OF HOURS OF CATHERINE OF CLEVES
(PIERPONT MORGAN LIBRARY), A PAINTING
BY PAOLO UCCELLO (NATIONAL GALLERY,
LONDON), AND THE BEST KNOWN RENDITION,
BY RAPHAEL. (CLICHÉ DES MUSÉES
NATIONAUX)

Prince of Darkness with one of his legs
lashed to an anvil, he extracted a solemn
promise never to menace a house over
whose entryway a horseshoe was nailed.
Satan had no choice but to accede to
Dunstan's blackmail. There is, all the
same, a loophole in the vow: only if the
shoe is hung with its open end facing upward will the charm prevail against all
the temptations of the devil. "Religion,"
writes Christopher Fry, "has made an
honest woman of the supernatural."

Another such wonder is attributed to
the seventh-century Bishop of Tournai
and Noyon, Saint Eligius (or Saint Eloi),
religious counselor to the "good" King
Dagobert, ruler of the Norman-domi-
nated Gauls. Like Saint Dunstan, Saint
Eloi was renowned for his craft as a metal-
worker. Unlike the Englishman, he was
not at all modest about his skill. His

hubris was such that he is said to have proclaimed himself the master of all smiths and farriers—and thus to have provoked the wrath of God, who dispatched Jesus to teach the arrogant Norman a lesson in humility. Christ appeared before the bishop's smithy in the guise of another blacksmith who disputed the cleric's claim. Eloi demanded that the stranger prove his skill by making a shoe for one of the king's most prized horses. Jesus complied in an astonishing manner: he severed the animal's leg, took careful measurements of the hoof, fabricated the shoe, nailed it in place, and restored the limb without the loss of a single drop of blood.

Nothing loath, Eloi sought to imitate Jesus' remarkable performance—with results that may be surmised. The horse bled so profusely that it would soon have perished. Great indeed were Eloi's remorse and contrition. Greater still, of course, was the compassion of Jesus. He re-attached the hacked-off leg and made the horse whole again. Recognizing his master (as well as his superior in craft), Eloi begged pardon for his boldness. In this way the saint, who was also a clever lapidary, became patron of all those who have anything to do with horses—in France.

ABOVE: THE VISION OF SAINT EUSTACE, *BY PISANELLO, PORTRAYS THE HOLY MAN WHO IS CONSIDERED THE PATRON SAINT OF THE HUNT IN WESTERN EUROPE. (NATIONAL GALLERY, LONDON) TOP LEFT:* SAINT GEORGE AND THE DRAGON *BY CARLO CRIVELLI. (NATIONAL GALLERY, LONDON) BOTTOM LEFT:* THE CONVERSION OF SAINT HUBERT *BY THE MASTER OF WERDEN. (NATIONAL GALLERY, LONDON)*

The Life, History and Magic of
THE HORSE

Donald Braider

GROSSET & DUNLAP
A FILMWAYS COMPANY
Publishers   New York

FOR HELEN BRAIDER, GRACE CLARK,
AND LAURIE DAVIS—HORSEWOMEN
ALL—WITH LOVE.

Published in 1973 by Grosset & Dunlap, Inc.,
New York

1978 PRINTING

Published simultaneously in Canada.
Library of Congress Catalog Card No.:
72–77107
ISBN: 0–448–02169–2
Printed in the United States of America

*Designed and produced by Chanticleer
Press, Inc., New York*

Contents

THE COMING OF EQUUS CABALLUS

Our subject is the horse, whose appearance on earth predates man's and who has been his invaluable companion and aide since the onset of recorded history. Work, sports, exploration, warfare—there is hardly an aspect of man's life in which the horse has not figured, and we recognize this fact in the frequency with which the animal appears in man's art and literature.

Most of the purely utilitarian functions once performed by the horse are now performed by machines, yet he retains for us his beauty and his special aura. This book, then, is devoted to him—to his life, history, and magic, and to all he has shared with man.

The Earliest Traces

Like man, *equus caballus* has resulted from a prolonged process of evolution. This history, unlike man's, is recorded with extraordinary fidelity and continuity in fossilized remains unearthed mainly in North America and northern Eurasia. The earliest evidences antedate those of *homo sapiens* by something like sixty million years.

Dates in this misty period of prehistory are almost hopelessly approximate. The epoch during which the first recognizable ancestor of the horse appeared is known as the Eocene, a period roughly spanning fifty-eight million B.C. to thirty-six million B.C. Hundreds of millions of years had already elapsed since the earth's beginnings. Plant life and animals had long since emerged from the sea and adapted themselves to the land with varying degrees of success. The Paleocene epoch, which had begun about sixty-three million B.C., had witnessed a gradual increase in the kinds and sophistication of plant and beast. These evolved and proliferated—reptile, bird, and plant alike—because the climate was warm and moist and thus exceptionally hospitable to the growth of all forms of life.

Undoubtedly, the horse had his ear-

6

*THE TWENTIETH-CENTURY
CHINESE PAINTER HSU PEI-
HUNG (JU PEON) CAPTURES THE
QUALITY OF WILDNESS THAT
CAN BE FOUND EVEN IN THE
TAMEST HORSE. (COLLECTION
ALICE BONEY, NEW YORK)*

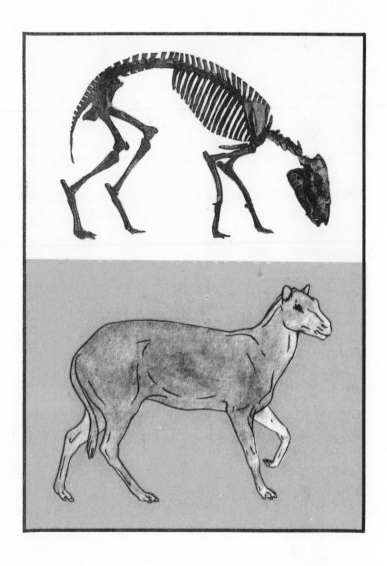

FOSSILIZED SKELETON OF EOHIPPUS, *THE EARLIEST ANCESTOR OF THE HORSE SO FAR UNEARTHED, TOGETHER WITH AN ARTIST'S RENDERING OF HOW HE MAY HAVE APPEARED. (AMERICAN MUSEUM OF NATURAL HISTORY, NEW YORK)*

liest antecedents in the Paleocene epoch. No related fossil from that period has, however, been discovered. But from the slightly more temperate climate of the Eocene, geologists have found fossilized skeletons of mammals whose descendants became *equus caballus.* These remains suggest a creature which even the most vivid imagination would have difficulty in relating to the marvel of flesh and bone we know today. The skeletal structure of two closely related animals have been unearthed from this long period—*phenacodus* and *eohippus.*

Phenacodus more nearly resembled a dog than a horse, with a small head, short ears, and a tail so long that it trailed on the ground. He was indigenous to Eurasia and the Americas. *Eohippus* was discovered in the 1890's, both in northern Europe and near the headwaters of the Mississippi River. Slightly taller than *phenacodus,* he was nevertheless comparatively small, ranging in height, at the equivalent of the withers, from 10 to 15 inches—about the size of a spring lamb ready for market. His skeleton, while bearing some resemblances to that of the modern horse, had remarkable extremities. The hind feet had three toes; the forefeet had four. In fleshy conformation, *eohippus* was like a tapir (to which he is related), notable for the upward arch of the neck and—if the naturalists' reconstruction is reliable—the forward angle at which his head was held and the tapering of the muzzle. His diet was mainly the succulent leaves of tropical vegetation and, consequently, his teeth were quite different from those of his descendants.

A slightly larger horselike animal inhabited North America perhaps ten million years into the Eocene epoch. This was *orohippus.* So far, his remains have been found only in the same region of the Mississippi's sources where *eohippus* was located. He was somewhat taller than his predecessor, with a slightly greater arch to his back, a characteristic that suggests he had adapted himself to feeding on the tall grasses of his marshy terrain. *Orohippus* differed from *eohippus* in two other respects: his teeth were flatter because of his food—more often grass than leaves; and his toes were less definitely articulated.

Mesohippus and Miohippus

At the end of the long Eocene epoch, about thirty-six million B.C., there seems to have been a more evolved creature in North America and Europe—*epihippus*. This species was probably wiped out in Europe by the horrendous floods of the Oligocene, an epoch that lasted fifteen million years. Because North America afforded the sanctuary of high ground on both sides of the Rocky Mountains, from western Canada to Texas and Baja California, it provided a haven and breeding ground for another form of evolving horse.

This new creature, *mesohippus*, was obviously an adaptation to the dramatic alterations of the habitat. Flooding had washed away the great jungle trees and shrubs, leaving, after the waters had receded and the ground had dried, vast expanses of grassy plains. Horses had to become grazers, like cattle. *Mesohippus* had about 4 inches in height over his immediate ancestor (which may have been either *eohippus* or *orohippus*). He had only three toes on each foot and a spinal column that was nearly horizontal—doubtless because he now had to escape from his natural enemies by virtue of speed and endurance rather than initial spring.

Toward the conclusion of the Oligocene, the modern horse's North American forebears went through a further change of structure in south-central Canada and near the Gulf of California. Evidences of *miohippus* have been found in these sectors. He stood approximately 28 inches at the withers and his rump rose 2 or 3 inches higher than that. Moreover, the lateral toes of forefeet and hind feet were of little use to him, since they no longer came in contact with the soil, which was now probably much firmer than it had been at the onset of the Oligocene epoch.

The origins of *miohippus* are believed to date from the very end of the Oligocene. It was in the Miocene, from which his name derives, that his importance was felt—not only in his native North America but in Asia and Europe, to which many of his numbers migrated and where they survived for eons. The principal strain of the modern horse, however, evolved from *mesohippus*. He continued to develop and flourish in North America and to migrate across the Bering Isthmus to Eurasia.

Further Modifications

Toward the end of the Miocene age, around thirteen million years ago, the horse's ancestors underwent further modifications. *Parahippus* was about 3 inches taller than *miohippus*, with forelegs that were straighter and a vertebral structure in which we can detect the earliest indications of the modern form of the withers. If zoologists are correct, the smooth coat of *parahippus* was striped, though not so markedly as that of the zebra, of which he may well have been an ancestor. He almost certainly migrated to Eurasia, but his remains have been discovered only in widely separated areas of North and Central America. Early in the Pliocene there evolved a taller variant of *parahippus*. This was *merychippus*, whose withers, about 36 inches from the ground, were more humped and whose dental structure was almost identical to that of *equus caballus*, the modern horse. His dun-colored coat and heavy head are much like those of several breeds of pony.

The most notable change in the horse during the Pliocene is the disappearance of the toes, which had long ago lost all utility. The earliest American species without toes is called *equus parvulus*; another is *hippidium*. Of somewhat later evolution were *equus pacificus* and *equus occidentalis*, both native to western America. All were monodactyl—having feet without toes. All were doomed to extinction in the New World.

Hipparion, discovered in several regions of Europe as well as in North America, is the subject of lively dispute.

Standing approximately 40 inches high, he was the last of the horse's ancestors to possess three toes, two of them useless. His coat is thought to have been striped, but in a less regular way than that of *parahippus*. In the opinion of some scientists, *hipparion* sired the onager, the donkey, and the zebra. Fossilized skeletons of this creature suggest to others, however, that he became extinct before the Pliocene epoch had run its course a million years ago.

In any event, it was *pliohippus* that most closely resembled the horse of today. About 5 inches taller than *hipparion*, *pliohippus* was the first of nature's true monodactyl creatures to survive. Gone were the superfluous toes, and though the bone formation of the legs was slender, its similarity to that of *equus caballus* was striking. Even more interesting, in the light of subsequent developments, is the fact that his remains have turned up exclusively in the southwestern United States and Central America as far south as Panama. But it is certain that he or his immediate descendants migrated in significant numbers to Eurasia. He surely sired the entire equine family of the Old World—*equus stenonis* and *equus quaggoides* of Italy, *hemionus fossilis* of Germany, *equus silvanensis* of Siberia, *equus nomadicus* of India, and *equus caballus* of Mongolia—the last, of course, the species of the modern horse.

What is inexplicable is the fact that none of the descendants of *pliohippus* survived the Pleistocene epoch in the New World. What killed them off, no one knows. But the horse was not alone in being eradicated from North and South America. So too were cattle of all varieties. The effect this would have

THOUGH MUCH LARGER THAN EOHIPPUS, MESOHIPPUS, IN THIS ARTIST'S IMPRESSION, IS STILL A FAR CRY FROM THE MODERN HORSE: SMALLER AND WITH THREE TOES. (AMERICAN MUSEUM OF NATURAL HISTORY, NEW YORK)

on human society in these immense areas would be devastating.

The Modern Horse Emerges

Pliohippus definitely sired one strain that flourished during the Pleistocene age (one million to around 10,000 B.C.). This creature was *plesihippus*, which was even larger than *equus caballus*. He stood 56 inches high (14 hands) and was powerfully boned and muscled. Had he survived the exceptionally harsh weather of the Pleistocene, he would undoubtedly have produced a race of horses much more impressive than those which evolved in Eurasia. However, *plesihippus* has left us only a solitary relic of his presence on earth, discovered in the celebrated La Brea Tar Pits of Los Angeles, California.

How prevalent his species was, or how long it endured, are matters still unclear to us.

Paralleling the career of *plesihippus* and outlasting it were those of various horselike creatures whose remains were unearthed all over Europe and Asia. The single survivor of these is *equus caballus*, another Pleistocene animal. Though his average height at the withers (about 52 inches) was less than that of *plesihippus*, he proved the hardiest and luckiest of the many offshoots of the long evolutionary lines of quadrupeds. *Equus caballus* is the progenitor of all horses; he was probably the only creature of the genus known to early man.

The skeletons of prehistoric horses found elsewhere in the Old World tell us that the differences between them

11

EOHIPPUS

MESOHIPPUS

MERYCHIPPUS

PLIOHIPPUS

Eocene period:
approximately 60 to 40 million
years B.C.

Height: 15 inches

Oligocene period:
40 to 25 million years B.C.

Height: 20½ inches

Miocene period:
approximately 25 to 10 million
years B.C.

Height: 35 inches

Pliocene period:
approximately 10 to
1 million years B.C.

Height: 44½ inches

EQUUS PRZEWALSKII

Pleistocene period:
approximately 1 million to 8,150 years B.C.

Height: 53 inches

and *equus caballus* were mainly those of size. *Equus caballus* existed at one time during the Pleistocene epoch in the Americas, for his bones have been found on both New World continents. But along with his bigger relation, *plesihippus*, he disappeared from the area during one of the epoch's thaws. He was not seen there again until the sixteenth Christian century, when the natives of Mexico first beheld him, carrying on his back one of the Spanish *conquistadores*.

Consequently, our consideration of the horse's history shifts from the lands where he seems to have originated to those where he migrated and proliferated. If *equus caballus* is unique in having escaped the modifications imposed by man's breeding and feeding and training of his relations, it is because one important herd was long lost in the Mongolian fastnesses and only discovered late in the last century by a Russian explorer after whom he was named: *equus prjewalskii*.

But other Pleistocene horses have adapted themselves to the terrains and climates to which their ancestors had come. In addition to those whose remains were found in Italy, Germany, Siberia, and Spain, others deserve mention. One is *equus giganteus*, which evolved in northern Europe and is probably the ancestor of the celebrated great horse that was bred in the Low Countries. The other is *equus scotti*, a creature of the arid, barren areas of North Africa and perhaps the sire of the Arabian. He was lean, swift, and compact. Thus, long before man evolved, nature had been at her work of selection, determining by the kind of land on which the horse was settled the sort of creature that would survive and multiply.

13

EARLY HORSE AND EARLY MAN

Early man was a hunter and a forager. Since the quarry he pursued and the fruits and vegetables and berries he sought were seasonal, he was also a nomad, a follower of the game and the natural harvests. In the beginning, man looked upon the horse merely as game. A herd of wild horses—descendants of primordial *equus caballus*, altered only in size, depending on the climate and terrain they occupied—would gradually be considered the preserve of a particular wandering tribe of humans. That tribe followed the horses, slaughtering them for food as required, unable to control their migrations, and therefore in a sense vassals of the horse, as of other game animals.

Eventually the tribes of hunters became tribes of herdsmen as well—even as today the Lapps maintain a loose but effective control over their herds of reindeer. As a given tribe came to understand the seasons and the terrain of its own territory a little better, it contrived to guide its herds to richer pastures. These amenable creatures, better nourished and protected against natural predators, multiplied at a rate that exceeded man's needs for food and became, in effect, savings, money in the bank, capital. Indeed, the word capital originates from the Latin *capite*, a head of livestock.

While horses grazed and became more numerous, tribal men and women took shelter in caves. It was on the walls of these dark dwellings that early humans (some anthropologists think they were women) left their first surviving sketches, those extraordinary pictures of the animals that sustained them. Art historians and archeologists have speculated widely and often wildly about the inspirations for these earliest works of art. Some tell us that the cave paintings of southwestern France, northern Spain, and North Africa—in all of which the horse figures prominently—were motivated by some primitive religious urge,

14

by magical thinking. Man imagined that if he could commit pictures of the horse and other game to the walls of his home (or were the caves actually temples?), he might in some arcane manner assure himself permanent possession of the herd and prevent it from straying from his tribe's territory.

This theory fails, however, to explain how widely-separated human societies could have devised virtually identical grammars of symbolism and forms of magic. A simpler hypothesis, and one that finds supporting evidence in surviving aboriginal cultures, is that there was a single ancient world civilization which spread such fundamentals. Apparently, when man's primal needs for food, shelter, and clothing had been satisfied, he had an impulse to create, to adorn. Magic and religion were doubtless products of later, somewhat more sophisticated societies.

Cave paintings and drawings attest to the fact that of all the creatures surrounding man, the horse proved the most useful, and that this was evident to humans in earliest recorded times. Man learned initially to halter and then to ride the horse. It would be thousands of years before he comprehended even the most elementary principles of selective breeding.

The original wild horses of Eurasia and North Africa wandered freely within the confines of territories to which they had adapted themselves naturally. Influences of climate, captivity, and eventually some rudimentary ideas about breeding dramatically changed the appearance of *equus caballus*. Men in any particular location were familiar only with the creature they had themselves domesticated. In fact, it was believed until 1879 that *equus caballus* was extinct, and had been for thousands of years. It was known that the various breeds of horse were descended from

him, but that he still existed in his first state was not suspected. In that spring, Captain Nicolai Prjewalski, a Russian explorer and amateur naturalist, came upon a herd of unfamiliar animals during a long journey on camelback through central Asia. His discovery caused a great deal of confusion at first—not least to the captain himself, who thought that he had found the primordial horse three years before. The matter was tentatively sorted out in 1881 by another Russian, the zoologist S. J. Polyakov, who named the animal *equus prjewalskii* (now *equus prjewalskii polyakov*). So far as can now be determined, this is *equus caballus* in his original condition.

A brief consideration of the living habits of this sturdy little creature (he stands about 12 to 14 hands) provides us with a clue to his capacity to survive, unchanged, severe hardships for something like one million years. The Mongolian or Siberian wild horse, as the breed

FROM MINOAN CYPRUS COMES THIS TERRACOTTA STATUETTE, DATING TO PERHAPS 1000 B.C., OF A HORSE WITH ACCOUTREMENTS, PROBABLY FOR RIDING. (METROPOLITAN MUSEUM OF ART, CESNOLA COLLECTION)

is often called, dwells in a most inhospitable upland region of Soviet Mongolia, a low range of sparsely vegetated, arid hills called the Ridge of the Yellow Horses (though the creatures' coats turn white in winter). His diet consists of tree branches, coarse grasses, and soft, tuberous roots. A group of the species is sheltered in the Prague zoo, and the Soviet government is purportedly doing its best to protect those in Mongolia from human depredations (they were treated as game by the natives of the region). In Germany, an interesting experiment in retrogressive breeding has succeeded in producing an animal very closely resembling the one that Captain Prjewalski discovered—this in order to demonstrate the validity of the theory that all horses are descended from that species.

The Horse Tamed

Exactly when it was that man learned he could domesticate the horse remains problematical. Also unknown is which of many human societies made the initial discovery. One theory is that the Chinese were the first horsemen. It is equally possible that the earliest were the aristocratic Brahmans of India. Hindu mythology sets its first human—variously called Manu, Sveyambhuva, or Viraj—

BELOW: A RELIEF DISCOVERED IN WESTERN ASIA MINOR SHOWS ONE OF THE EARLIEST REPRESENTATIONS OF HORSES HARNESSED TO A CHARIOT. (BIBLIOTHÈQUE NATIONALE, PARIS)
OPPOSITE: THE GREAT ASSYRIAN CITY OF NINEVEH, REDISCOVERED IN THE LAST CENTURY, YIELDED THIS RELIEF OF WILD HORSES BEING HUNTED BY MEN USING ARROWS AND DOGS. (BRITISH MUSEUM)

astride a horse whose every part and member symbolizes some aspect of man's nature or condition. Since Manu, in the Brahman tradition, was the author of the code by which all faithful Hindus of the earliest epoch were supposed to live, it seems fair to infer that mastery of equitation was regarded as a very significant achievement in this ancient civilization.

But there is no evidence that the horse of Brahman India was an object of worship. The creature seems, rather, to have represented earthly life and man's capacity to control his natural environment. The horse was also identified with the practices of war. The first tribe of any region to ride a horse with some self-assurance was probably the one which dominated its less competent neighbors. The horse was also a vital asset in hunting. Both of these occupa-

19

THIS ASSYRIAN RELIEF OF BATTLE
CHARIOTS PULLED BY HORSES IS
ONE OF THE EARLIEST DEPICTIONS
OF THE HORSE AT WAR. (CLICHÉ
DES MUSÉES NATIONAUX)

tions were masculine; rare indeed is an early pictorial representation of a woman on horseback.

If the Brahmans were the first to master the horse, they were not alone for very long in this role. Equitation was a discipline soon acquired by peoples in every corner of the earth where horses were to be found—in Asia, North Africa, and Europe. Chinese, Assyrians, and Persians were skilled riders in the third millennium B.C.. In China, as far as we now know, only the mandarins and their cavalrymen were equestrians. There and surely elsewhere, the horse was ridden before he became a draft animal. It is probable that in these earliest major civilizations, the powerful but phlegmatic bovines were found more tractable for drawing vehicles or agricultural implements.

The harness necessary for such work is believed to be an invention of about 4000 B.C. It consisted at first of a wooden yoke attached by rope to the object drawn. The secret of the harness was the cordage, and no one knows when this material was first made or where. Nor do we know with what kind of fibers the earliest rope was fashioned. Perfecting rope has been compared in importance with the development of sails, which it must have preceded, since no sailing craft could be managed without the use of lines. A Persian miniature bronze of about 2800 B.C. depicting a war chariot drawn by four onagers suggests that the use of horses as draft animals may have followed soon afterwards.

Luigi Gianoli, whose researches on the horse in earliest antiquity are without peer, suggests that the Chinese were perhaps the first civilized men to ride *and* to harness the horse. In his excellent book,

Horses and Horsemanship through the Ages, Gianoli cites Chinese ceramic representations of ridden and harnessed horses, dated at about 3500 B.C.

The horse figured significantly in oriental mythology, a key to its cultural importance. It seems probable that the Orientals learned to harness horses before they learned to ride them. Credit for being the first equestrian culture belongs in all likelihood to the nomadic tribes of Asia Minor, but this is pure surmise, predicated on the theory that herdsmen have more need to ride than do farmers. Certain it is, nevertheless, that the Chinese made use of the horse earlier, to a greater extent, and in more ways than did any other civilization. There was hardly a modern use of the animal that was not known to this people a full millennium before the Christian era. Moreover, the Chinese were skilled in selective breeding. They had several kinds of horses for different applications.

Little of this intelligence could have filtered across the immense distance of mountains and deserts and steppes that separates China from the Mediterranean. The Thracians, the Ionians, the Sumerians, the Hittites, and the Assyrians gradually mastered the horse on their own. It is to the Hittites that we owe the first extant text on the care and rearing of horses, a cuneiform document written about 1600 B.C. So meticulous a work could only be the product of a civilization that had put the horse to use in the manner that man knows best and perfects most eagerly—war. The Hittites, with the assistance of horse-drawn chariots, defeated their neighbors as far south as the Euphrates (The carts, it should be noted, were originally of Sumerian design). "The

scalp of your enemy is progress," wryly observed the Irish writer, James Stephens.

The better-documented culture of Assyria discloses the relevance of the horse to the spread of that people's influence throughout Asia Minor. It also seems that the Assyrians were the first of the eastern Mediterranean cultures to make use of an article resembling a saddle, suggesting an adaptation made necessary by the great distances covered by their armies. When they were not making war, the Assyrians used their riding horses for hunting. The tack employed was crude but it was surprisingly complete, including a device very like the modern standing martingale, which prevents the horse from throwing his head too high. All that the Assyrians lacked was the stirrup, but since no one

else had such an asset at the time, it was not missed. Their appreciation of the role of the horse is reflected in the epitaph Darius, one of their great kings, composed for himself: "I loved my friends, was an excellent horseman, an excellent hunter, and found nothing impossible." For all but the first of these assertions, Darius owed everything to mastery of the horse.

The Egyptians first tamed and used the horse at the onset of the eighteenth dynasty—the epoch of the "new empire" (from about 1650 B.C. onward), when the incestuous rulers of the Nile delta were extending their dominion in all directions. Curiously, the people of this wonderful civilization evinced no interest in equitation. For them, the horse was solely a draft animal. He pulled the light, fast, two-wheeled chariots to

battle in the manner employed by the Assyrians more than a thousand years earlier. He hauled the lazy Egyptians to the hunt. The beasts on whose backs men crossed the deserts of Arabia and North Africa were the camel, the dromedary, and occasionally the ox— or so we are led to believe by the sculptures, illustrations, hieroglyphs, and artifacts coming down to us from ancient Egypt.

Yet this is difficult to believe, for the civilizations of Babylonia and Assyria roughly contemporaneous with that of the eighteenth Egyptian dynasty were using horses not only for war but for sport, and were experimenting with breeding techniques. The horses of Babylon and Nineveh do not for a moment foreshadow the magnificent Arabians we know today. What we recognize, however, is clearly a much sleeker animal than the Siberian wild horse.

Early Mythology

The horse entered the recorded annals of western culture in the same way as so many other phenomena—through mythology. Greek myths about the horse are nonetheless astonishing, for the animal was imagined to be the creation of the water god Poseidon, and to have emerged originally from the sea. Perhaps this myth originates in the attack on a Mediterranean island by an enemy force; Crete suggests itself because it was there that the horse made its first appearance to the Minoans, in the final phase of their hold on that island in the second millennium B.C. The assualt craft would have carried horses as well as soldiers. When the fleet was still at some distance from the island's beach, the cavalrymen could have mounted their steeds and ridden rapidly ashore, easily overwhelming the awed defenders

who knew of no way to contend with so alarming a combination of man and beast.

Such an occurrence would explain not only the myth of the horse originating in the sea, but also that extraordinary figure of the primitive imagination, the centaur—a creature half-man, half-horse. Once victorious, the invading soldiers on horseback may well have carried off the women of the conquered island—and hence the myth of the powerful and lustful centaurs.

Perhaps the first sight of a horse galloping through the shallow water, kicking up a white foam as does the prow of a boat, gave rise to the conception of the winged wonder-horse, Pegasus. Whatever his origin in fact, Pegasus in Greek mythology was a wild creature, untamed and untamable by normal processes. When Athene, the chaste goddess of wisdom, looked with favor on the mortal warrior Bellerophon, she appeared to him in a vision and enabled him to behead Medusa and to conquer

THE LID OF A BRONZE ETRUSCAN BURIAL URN OF THE FIFTH OR SIXTH CENTURY B.C. DEPICTS A SCYTHIAN HORSEMAN. (METROPOLITAN MUSEUM OF ART, JOSEPH PULITZER BEQUEST)

25

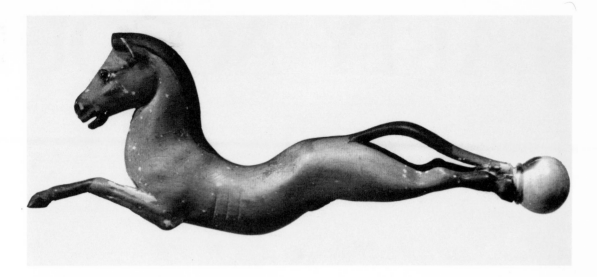

LEFT: A ROMAN MOSAIC, THOUGHT TO BE OF THE THIRD CENTURY A.D., REFERS TO THE MYTH OF POSEIDON AND HIS WIFE, AMPHITRITE, IN WHICH THE HORSE FIGURES SIGNIFICANTLY. (CLICHÉ DES MUSÉES NATIONAUX)

ABOVE: A PRANCING HORSE, CARVED IN IVORY ON THE HANDLE OF AN EGYPTIAN WHIP OF THE FOURTEENTH CENTURY B.C. (METROPOLITAN MUSEUM OF ART, CARNARVON COLLECTION)

the Gorgons. On this occasion, Athene handed Bellerophon a golden bridle. With this treasure, he was able to ride Pegasus—thereby becoming, according to the Greek canon, the first of mortal horsemen.

Pegasus also appeared in Greek mythology as Poseidon's means of disclosing the sources of fresh water to man. The hoofbeats of the winged horse aroused the waters of the sacred spring Hippocrene and caused them to gush forth. Perhaps, here again, there is an elementary logic underlying the superstition, for we know that the primordial Siberian wild horse rediscovered by Prjewalski paws the earth in summertime at points he instinctively or empirically knows to be waterholes.

Oddly, we find that in graphic, sculptural, and literary representations of Greek beliefs, it is not Pegasus but the centaurs that are, literally, the fountainheads—protectors of the precious springs that quench man's thirst. It was probably the horse's ability (transferred to the mythical centaur) to find sources of water which led the Greeks to believe

that centaurs were repositories of other wisdom as well. The centaur Chiron was tutor of Castor and Pollux and of Heracles.

Attributing great wisdom to such a creature is not uniquely Greek. The Chinese had a similar conviction and carried the notion of the centaur's intellectual preeminence one step further. The mandarins believed that a mythical race, the Ting-Ling, who were remarkably like the centaurs of the Greeks, were the sagest of all beings. The Ting-Ling inhabited Formosa, which suggests that they and the centaurs may have had their legendary origins in similar island occurrences—an invasion from the mainland.

The horse's position in mythology, wherever he figures at all, is associated with wisdom, power, and, above all, utility. If it is true, as many archeologists increasingly argue, that myth is history dimly remembered, the role of the horse in mythology—invariably a happy one —is easy to understand as a reflection of his role in the development of civilization.

27

EARLY ACCOUNTS

IT MAKES MEN IMPERIOUS TO SIT A HORSE.
THE AUTOCRAT OF THE BREAKFAST
TABLE,—OLIVER WENDELL HOLMES

We have mentioned that it was the Hittites who first produced a manual describing the proper management of the horse. Their cuneiform, however, was not a language the Greeks could master, even had they discovered the clay tablets on which the information was inscribed. Nevertheless, they may have obtained the essentials of Hittite and Assyrian wisdom by observation or by word of mouth. To these they added what they had learned by trial and error.

Simon of Athens, Xenophon, and Alexander the Great

There were two important works on the subject available to owners and trainers of horses before 400 B.C. The earlier by about a generation was written by one Simon of Athens, a professional horse manager. Of this work only a single chapter and some fragments remain to us. Yet in his own day, Simon gained so much esteem that, when he died, a bronze sculpture in his honor was erected in Attica's principal city. Simon's surviving chapter deals mainly with the horse's anatomy. He advises his reader what to look for in a colt's conformation, and what he has to say is of interest not merely for its common sense but also for his description of the ideal horse. Luigi Gianoli observes that Simon's characterization evokes a horse very like the Arabian. One suspects, however, that such an animal was not often seen in Athens in the author's era. Like the superb, ideal woman created by Praxiteles in marble, Simon's perfect horse was a phenomenon—not the run-of-the-mill creature found in Greece. Were there Arab horses in Attica at this early time? They do not appear in the sculpture of the period. Certainly there were not many, and certainly they did not perpetuate themselves into the Hellenistic epoch, when Rome mastered and emulated all it found admirable in Greek civilization.

Xenophon, the Greek poet, has be-

PRECEDING PAGE: A COIN FROM
HELLENISTIC SYRACUSE DEPICTS
A TWO-HORSE CHARIOT. THE USE
OF THE HORSE ON COINAGE
SUGGESTS THE ANIMAL'S
IMPORTANCE IN THIS
CIVILIZATION. (BIBLIOTHÈQUE
NATIONALE)

queathed to us the first complete *Treatise on Equitation* which has come down through the millennia more or less intact. Not only a poet, Xenophon was also a soldier and a passionate admirer of horses. He was a friend of Sparta's king Agesilaus, with whom he rode into battle. Although Xenophon was unexpectedly deprived of his cavalry rank and exiled, he was allowed to settle near Olympia, scene of the games after which the modern Olympics are named. There he compiled the first serious essays on the horse, in which he set down his thoughts on the philosophy of horsemanship and the psychology of the horseman—in part from the horse's point of view as he conceived it:

The hand must be neither held so strict as to confine and make the horse uneasy, nor so loosely as not to let him feel it. The moment he obeys and answers it, yield the bridle to him; this will take off the stress and relieve his bars [bits], and is in conformity with that maxim, which should not be forgot, which is to caress and reward him for whatever he does well. The moment the rider perceives that the horse begins to place his head, to go lightly in the hand, and with ease and pleasure to himself, [the rider] should do nothing that is disagreeable, but flatter and coax, suffer him to rest a while, and do all he can to keep [the horse] in his happy temper. This will encourage and prepare him for greater undertakings.

[Anonymous English translation, 1802]

Wholly admirable are Xenophon's understanding of the principle of winning and keeping the confidence of the horse and particularly his disquisition on the soft use of the rider's hands.

It is evident from the writings of such authors as Homer and Aristotle that the Hellenes employed the horse in every conceivable fashion. But it was undoubt-

edly the animal's value on the field of battle that won him his most memorable place in history. Twenty years or so after Xenophon's death, in the early years of the fourth century B.C., there arose in nearby Macedonia one of the greatest military geniuses of the ancient world— Alexander the Great. From the time he was ten, the boy was tutored by Aristotle in the arts of kingship and by his royal father, Philip, in the arts of war and leadership in battle. He surely learned to ride at an early age, hunted at Philip's side, watched the races at Olympia, and became an accomplished equestrian.

Alexander acceded to the throne of Macedonia at the age of twenty. Shortly afterward, he secured his late father's other, more symbolic position as ruler of the League of Corinth. His achievements during the thirteen years that remained to him were astonishing—and so they still appeared twenty-one centuries later to Napoleon Bonaparte, who took Alexander for his ideal.

What Alexander accomplished so spectacularly, he accomplished principally on horseback. One Hellenistic bronze sculpture of the great young conqueror, which was found in the volcanic ash that engulfed the ancient city of Herculaneum, shows the emperor astride Bucephalus, the horse that had carried him since his twelfth year. According to tradition, Alexander so loved Bucephalus that he commemorated the animal's death by creating a new town, Bucephala, not far from the better-known city of Nicaea. It is one of the few instances of a human community named for a horse.

Yet it was absolutely proper that Alexander should not only honor Bucephalus, but through him pay tribute to all the horses which participated in the dizzying series of conquests that marked his brief career. There can be

LEFT: THE POPULARITY OF THE HORSE IN THE DAILY LIFE OF THE GREEKS IS SEEN IN A DETAIL FROM A CRATER (VASE) OF ABOUT THE FIFTH CENTURY B.C. (CLICHÉ DES MUSÉES NATIONAUX)
RIGHT: A DETAIL FROM A GREEK AMPHORA OF AN ANCIENT VERSION OF THE CIRCUS IS ONE OF THE EARLIEST KNOWN REPRESENTATIONS OF THE HORSE IN ENTERTAINMENT. (BIBLIOTHÈQUE NATIONALE)

no accurate estimate of the number in the emperor's cavalry. The memoirs of Ptolemy and Aristobulus, two of his most trusted lieutenants, have it that when he crossed the Hellespont, Alexander was riding at the head of 30,000 foot soldiers and 5,000 cavalrymen. He is reported to have had as many as 8,000 men on horseback later on in this same campaign. The figure would be more impressive were it not for records that his enemies had as many as 30,000 horsemen.

Consequently, if any credence is to be accorded these figures (which they probably do not merit), Alexander's success was not attributable to sheer numbers, but to the way in which he deployed his cavalry, a method that became classic. Mounted soldiers were used to strike the initial blow against

enemy lines—a frontal assault to throw the opponents into confusion. The cavalry also attempted to outflank the opposition, to cut off possible lines of retreat, to separate an army from its sources of supply. After Alexander, warfare was never the same, and the face of the Mediterranean world was irrevocably altered. Whether or not the young emperor was the chosen instrument of the gods, as he elected to believe, it is certain that the horse was the key to his numerous victories.

The bronze statuette of Alexander astride Bucephalus is thought to have been copied from a work in marble by Lysippus, a contemporary of Alexander. Especially interesting is the conformation of the horse and the details of its trappings. By modern standards, Bucephalus was a pony. If he was modelled in pro-

32

portion to his rider, he probably stood no more than 14 hands. There is almost certainly some distortion in the delineation of the animal's torso, which is inordinately elongated.

But for sleekness and muscularity and obvious agility, we cannot deny that Bucephalus was the result of prolonged refinement of breeding, training, and diet. He is still a long way from resembling the legendary horse of the Arabs, but we can see the direction in which his descendants would go. As for the tack, it consisted of a simple saddle blanket, probably of padded leather and secured by a girth and chest strap. The bridle lacks reins, but these were probably lost in the process of exhumation; what remains resembles a plain halter with a very small bit. The horses of Greece and Rome were, for some centuries after-

ward, very much like the little creature of the Herculaneum bronze—compact, well-muscled, and hardy. In addition, there were other animals of stouter conformation intended for heavier work, since breeding techniques were making rapid progress.

The Gauls and the Romans

Hardly less awesome than the achievement of Alexander in the Near East was the Gallic conquest of northern and western Europe; and the Gauls surely owed most of their success—at least in terms of the speed with which this was accomplished—to the horse. Their mounts were of a much heavier and sturdier stock than those of the Greeks and Romans, for they were raised in a climate that was at once more severe and more productive of lusher vegeta-

tion. The Gallic horses were the ancestors of the draft animals the Romans would cherish when they in their turn had conquered Gaul.

Apart from their powerful horses, the Gauls were remarkable for their ingenuity in constructing vehicles substantial enough to traverse pathless terrain without constantly falling apart. Their first contact with Rome took place about 600 B.C., when they occupied the Po Valley. Their rule was brief, for as soon as Rome had subdued her more immediate neighbors, the Etruscans and the Greeks, she undertook to master the people of adjacent territories. In the process, the Romans adopted those practices, arts, artifacts, and livestock-breeding customs which they considered useful to the furtherance of their main aim—empire.

It is probably only a slight exaggeration to describe the Romans as the magpies of the ancient world. They borrowed and stole ideas and tastes from every source to which they had access. This debt is evident in their friezes, paintings, sculptures, and literature. Nowhere is this talent for adaptation more evident than in the use, breeding, and deployment of the horse. Rome's most significant use of the horse was, not surprisingly, in war. Combining eastern cavalry techniques with the transport

methods of the Gauls, Latium launched itself upon the known world with a single-mindedness of purpose that was for a very long time invincible.

But the battle of Adrianopolis in A.D. 378 was the beginning of the end for Rome. Gothic cavalry achieved against Roman infantry what the Gauls (and the Huns, for that matter) had never been able to do—a slaughter of foot soldiers virtually at will. It is astonishing to discover that Latium never fully appreciated what Alexander had grasped 700 years before: the devastating effect on morale of calvary charges aimed not so much at gaining ground as at disrupting communications and disorienting troops. The Goths made use of mounted forces in a fashion we would now call guerrilla warfare.

By this time, the grandeur that was Rome had shifted to Constantinople, to that sector of Christendom called Byzantium. The Eastern emperors rapidly mastered what their Western predecessors had been too complacent to learn—to fight fire with fire. The role of cavalry in Byzantium was crucial to the defense of the Eastern Roman Empire. All of its enemies were mounted, so protection against them was also provided by mounted men. Until the final quarter of the eleventh century, this defensive posture served Byzantium well. In 1071, the emperor Romanus IV Diogenes committed imperial forces to the offense against the Turks at Manzikert, in Armenia. He himself was captured, his army of 60,000 men, at least half of it cavalry, was wiped out, and the fall of

Constantinople in 1453 was the inevitable finale. Thereafter, Islam dominated the Near East.

The Horse of the Koran

When God created the horse, he said to the magnificent creature: "I have made thee unlike any other. All the treasures of the earth lie between thine eyes. Thou shalt cast mine enemies between thy hooves, but thou shalt carry my friends on thy back. This shall be the seat from which prayers rise unto me. Thou shalt find happiness all over the earth, and thou shalt be favored above all other creatures, for to thee shall accrue the love of the master of the earth. Thou shalt fly without wings and conquer without sword."

The KORAN (An English translation, London, 1880)

Thus spoke Allah through his prophet Mohammed. One line is striking for its similarity to the conceptions of the Brahmans, the Chinese, and the Greeks: "All the treasures of the earth lie between thine eyes." This attribution of a special magic to the horse, whether traceable to more ancient civilizations or embedded in Arabian folklore, is evidence of the high place the horse occupied in Islamic culture from its onset.

It is likely that the horse referred to so often in the Koran was an Arab, or at any rate one of the immediate ancestors of that remarkable breed. For whatever the animals of the northern Mediterranean areas possessed in sturdiness, they were much less than "magnificent." Origins of the Arab horse are obscure.

35

Ammianus Marcellinus, a Roman historian of the fourth Christian century, who picked up the narrative of Rome's history where Tacitus had allowed it to drop, makes fleeting reference to the speed and endurance of the horses ridden by the Saracens, but there is little reason to assume that these creatures were Arabs, though of course they were descended from the noble creatures of Assyria, desert horses tempered by the arduous climate and arid terrain of the Near East.

The consensus is that the horse which carried Islam all the way from Mecca to Poitiers, in France, taking barely a century to accomplish this military wonder, was an animal bred by the Bedouin tribes of Arabia. It was a beast of Spartan temperament and will, whose very survival under such atrocious conditions made him a treasure. Perhaps in

the most demanding and rapid evolutionary phase, when man and horse became absolutely essential to each other's existence, the intimate and special relationship between them was at last firmly established—a mystique which endures.

However, the prophet Mohammed's prognosis for the horse's exalted future, reflected in the initial portion of the quotation from the Koran, was not wholly accurate. The horse would not always conquer, nor would he be easily conquered. Unlike the cat and the dog, creatures finally born tame after countless centuries of service and affinity to man, each successive generation of horses has to be domesticated, one by one. Every colt and filly, regardless of its aristocratic lineage, must be subjected to its master's will. The process is called breaking. It is not a misnomer.

THE HORSE IN MEDIEVAL LIFE AND MYTH

RIDER AND HORSE—FRIEND AND FOE—IN ONE RED BURIAL BLENT!
CHILDE HAROLD, *LORD BYRON*

This chapter will attempt to account for the developing and often confusing relationship between "rider and horse, —friend, foe" as the two antagonists joined their efforts. If it sometimes seems contradictory, it is because man was not always certain where he stood in relation to his indispensable ally, the horse, to which he at times ascribed supernatural powers and which, at others, he scorned and maltreated. The Middle Ages, moreover, were characterized by such confusions; at their conclusion, man lost God and found himself. So overwhelming a change of outlook was bound to have a distressing influence on the outline of history—not least as it concerned the horse.

The Arabian Steed

Like so many other events of the remote past, the ancestry of the Arab horse rests more on legend than on ascertainable fact. Islam and Judaism have contributed jointly to the fabulous annals

of this creature's development. The Arabian steed is said to have originated with the nomadic Bedouins who, if we believe the Bible, were descendants of the outcast Ishmael. It is to Ishmael, who had to learn first how to survive in the desert, that tradition ascribes the first inbreeding that produced the hardy and nervy Arab horse. Ishmael captured a wild mare which was in foal. He tamed her and mated her with her stallion son. This mare, Kuhaylan, gave her name to an increasingly refined series of horses which we know as the primordial Arab. So goes one of the tales.

The Bible also records that among other tributes which the beautiful Queen of Sheba brought to King Solomon were horses descended from Ishmael's Kuhaylan. According to this account, it was thus that the horse of Arabia began to improve the breeds of other regions of the Near East.

The chronicles of Mohammed tell us that the prophet maintained a large herd

38

Hubcati epilcopi et conf. Ant
te landus digne ad memoria

of trained horses. He subjected them to the following test: About one hundred animals were deprived of water for three full days and then were freed from the enclosure where they had been confined. All naturally rushed toward the nearest watering place, but hardly had Mohammed released them when he ordered the horn of battle to be blown. Wild with thirst, almost all the mares continued galloping toward water and paid no attention to the summons. But five came abruptly to a halt and dutifully responded to the prophet's call, trotting back to his side. Having proved themselves to be improbably obedient, this little group of five mares was singled out for Mohammed's blessing. They were known thereafter as "the five mares of the Prophet," and became the most cherished dams of Islam. (By contrast, Mohammed is known to have shown special favor to only one stallion, named Borak.) The mares foaled the finest of all Arab stock, and from this group derived the only strain of Arab horses that could legitimately carry the name of *asil*—animals of pure blood.

Whatever truth lies behind these accounts, it is indisputable that the Bedouin herdsmen, who often hired themselves out as cavalrymen to whatever chieftain or princeling offered the highest proportion of booty, bred for this purpose horses of uncommon beauty, stamina, and speed. It is equally plain that the spread of Islam was accomplished on horseback. For this reason, Mohammedanism was disseminated much more rapidly than Christianity.

It would be difficult to exaggerate the role of the horse in the history of Islam, and it is understandable that the Moslems treated foals with a care that bordered on idolatry. Until the time for

PRECEDING PAGE: INTERPRETATION OF THE CONVERSION OF SAINT HUBERT, FROM THE BOOK OF HOURS OF CATHERINE OF CLEVES. (PIERPONT MORGAN LIBRARY)   ABOVE: A HUNT AND BATTLE ARE DEPICTED IN THIS DETAIL OF A 16TH-CENTURY INDIAN MINIATURE. (VICTORIA AND ALBERT MUSEUM). OPPOSITE: THE ZOROASTRIANS GOING DOWN TO DEFEAT AT THE HANDS OF ISLAMIC CAVALRYMEN IN THIS THIRTEENTH CENTURY PERSIAN MINIATURE. (VICTORIA AND ALBERT MUSEUM)

their training began, colts and fillies were nurtured by the women of each community. Their normal diet was supplemented with eggs, dates, and camel's milk. When it was available, crushed barley was added to this wholesome regime. The animals were not just closely watched over, but were made to share the daily life of the tribe, the theory being that they would thus become accustomed to noises and gestures that might otherwise distract them on the field of battle.

One curiosity of the Arab horse's education probably resulted from the proximity of the dromedary: it usually knelt in order to facilitate mounting. Some

horses, we are told, refused food from any hand but their master's. One of the most interesting breeding customs of the Islamic horsemen is that they appear to have kept records only of their mares. When the three stallions which constituted the foundation strains of the Thoroughbred in England were placed at stud, no records at first were maintained of the mares they serviced— just the reverse of the Mohammedan practice. The foals of the mares of the prophet were treasured; rarely were they exported. Their principal purpose was to strengthen the native stock.

In the year A.D. 732, barely a century after the death of Mohammed, the

Moslems reached Poitiers in France. Tradition set the battle that took place there between the apparently invincible followers of the Islamic prophet and the decadent Merovingian Franks at nearby Tours. It is not altogether definite that it was the superiority of the Moorish cavalry that brought Islam so far so quickly. Their equipment certainly helped; their saddles were equipped with stirrups, devices unknown to the western Europeans. Yet at Poitiers they lost to a Frankish cavalry whose armor was proof against Islam's swords and spears. The Moors retreated to the northern slopes of the Pyrenees, but their failure to maintain a hold in France did not prevent them from leaving an influence there, especially in terms of the breeding and employment of horses.

In Spain, where they continued to prosper for many harmonious centuries, the Moslems left a powerful mark on the country's history. The influence of Moorish horses on the breeds already developed in Iberia were of great significance when the rulers Fernando and Isabel reunited Spain under the sign of the cross—and also when Spain reintroduced horses in the New World, horses that were Spanish-bred but Arab-influenced.

The Moslem horse, saddle, stirrup, style of riding, and technique of cavalry

43

RIGHT: JOUSTING, A FAVORITE SPORT OF MEDIEVAL NOBILITY IN NORTHERN EUROPE, IS ILLUSTRATED IN AN ILLUMINATED MANUSCRIPT. (BRITISH MUSEUM)

OVERLEAF: A PAINTING BY GIOVANNI DE FRANCESCO TOSCANI DEPICTS THE PALIO, AN ANNUAL HORSE RACE THROUGH THE STREETS OF RENAISSANCE FLORENCE. (DETAIL, CLEVELAND MUSEUM OF ART, HOLDEN COLLECTION)

on couste sanz conque auesse

ONE OF THE MOST CELEBRATED WORKS BY THE GREAT DUTCH
MASTER, REMBRANDT, IS THE POLISH RIDER. (FRICK COLLECTION,
NEW YORK)

The Knight's Mount

The first of the Holy Roman Emperors had learned a good deal about horsemanship during his encounters with the Moors, whom he drove across the Pyrenees back into Spain. In the millennium that followed, massed cavalry was a major feature of almost every important land battle fought by Europeans. The most famous of medieval cartoon strips, the Bayeux tapestry, shows the vital role of the horse in the Norman conquest of Britain. During subsequent centuries of war, the horse played a part second only to that of man himself.

As the accompanying illustrations prove, the demands placed on the horse were many. Some of them were epic. As war became more sophisticated, the

equipment of the average horseman became heavier. So the horse that carried him had to be bred to a larger size. From the First Crusade at the end of the eleventh century onward, an epoch which saw the dawn of European chivalry (a term which itself originates in the French word for horse), the horse and his rider came more and more to resemble in appearance and purpose the tank in the wars of our own time. This was not, as we shall see, so much a discovery as a rediscovery. The arts of chivalry and the armor of war long antedated the medieval era.

The important difference between the horse and the armored vehicle, of course, is that the former is mortal. Almost every cavalry manual from every land,

LEFT: A BLACKSMITH SHOEING A HORSE, AN UNUSUAL SCENE FROM A MEDIEVAL ILLUMINATED MANUSCRIPT. (BRITISH MUSEUM)
BELOW: A KNIGHT, FROM THE ILLUMINATED ADDRESS OF ROBERT D'ANJOU, NORMAN CONQUEROR OF SICILY AND SOUTHERN ITALY. (BRITISH MUSEUM)

including that of the ancient Hittites, contains this admonition to the soldier: "Kill the horse." Modern artillery orders similarly propose the destruction or disablement of the tank. The knight, like the occupant of the tank, was trebly vulnerable when deprived of his means of transport.

The proportions and brute strength of the medieval great horse which was bred to carry the fully-armored cavalier are awesome. The archetype of the epoch is surely the Ardennes, described later on in this book. The armor of the knight was so heavy that its wearer in many cases was unable to stand up in it without assistance. He could be set astride his mount (the horse itself frequently caparisoned with material of even greater weight) only by means of some sort of hoist.

The combined burden of rider and armor could easily exceed 700 pounds. A normal riding horse could carry such a load only briefly and for a short distance at a slow gait. To bear it for hours and at speed, and to be able to maneuver effectively when in close and dangerous quarters, demanded a truly remarkable creature. And so, even today, the numerous descendants of the great horse are astonishing for their tractability, agility, speed, and endurance.

The city of Venice still celebrates, in its greatest annual festival, the prowess of the fabulous horse Bucentaur, which carried knights to the Crusades. Venice still pays tribute to the horse which bore the Crusaders where no Venetian vessel could pass.

More interesting by far than the techniques of breeding that were finally to produce such giants as the Percherons, Shires, and Clydesdales is the manner in which man taught this early battle horse to respond to commands that were totally alien to the gentle equine nature. The horse, as we have noted, is temperamentally a creature of the herd, timid and without aggressive tendencies. How have trainers managed over the centuries to induce horses to brave the terrible sounds and strife of battle and to do so apparently without losing any of the sweetness that is normal to them?

This has evidently been managed in part by selective breeding. There are some horses, however, that cannot be induced, no matter how tasty the carrot proffered, to enter the noisy, smoky, hazardous field of battle. But to those

SAINT LOUIS, KING OF FRANCE, DEPARTING FOR THE SEVENTH CRUSADE, AN ILLUSTRATION FROM THE CHRONIQUES DE SAINT DENIS, A MEDIEVAL HISTORY OF FRANCE. (BRITISH MUSEUM)

animals that could be persuaded to heed their masters' commands, it is clear that the devils they knew—their trainers—were more menacing than the ones they did not know. Horses are much more easily intimidated by the certainty of punishment for failure to obey a command than by the prospect that confronts them in battle. They obviously cannot know that survival in their first venture into combat merely prepares them for the second, and so on. The horse does not fear death. Indeed, so far as we know, no animal except man has any conception at all of death. The horse's fear is inspired by an apprehension of pain and by an instinct to preserve himself. The process of preparing a horse for battle is one of conditioning (or, rather, of reconditioning) his reflexes—and it is not very lovely to contemplate. To understand the methods employed, we have only to

inspect some of the appalling bits that have been used through the ages.

Horseshoe, Bit, Saddle, and Stirrup

There was some concern about the safety of the horse in war. For one thing, he represented a substantial investment of time, energy, and money. Not all the bits used were cruel and not all the spurs had three-inch spines. Moreover, it must have been at a fairly early stage of western civilization that man realized the need to protect the hoof. The first examples of horseshoes that we know are Roman. They resembled wrought-iron sandals; they were affixed more or less permanently to the hoof by flanges which were clamped into place while the metal was still malleable.

It could not have been many centuries later that the first farrier discovered that the hornlike tissue of the exterior portion of the hoof was nerveless and could have nails driven into it without injuring the creature's foot. The nailed horseshoe was as revolutionary an invention as the pneumatic tire for the automobile, for it made possible much longer and more rapid journeys carrying heavier burdens. Even over short distances, the shoe reduced wear and damage to the soft hoof and to the bones of the leg, whether the load was being carried on the horse's back or was harnessed to him. With the development of the paved road in later Roman days, the horseshoe assumed an even greater importance. Although few roads were paved in that era, these included the arteries utilized by larger horsedrawn vehicles.

The invention of the bit, as we have remarked, came long before that of the shoe. It may even have antedated the iron age, although the earliest bits known to us are made of iron. The jointed snaffle was in general use throughout Asia Minor from about 1500 B.C. onward. In the age of Xenophon, at least two bits were employed, one composed of "wide little disks" that was for tractable horses, the other with "a sharp and pointed mouthpiece," rather like the modern curb bit, for the recalcitrant ones. Xenophon does not mention a bit resembling the snaffle.

Though surviving examples of the bits employed over the centuries indicate how many devices were invented to govern the horse at the point where he is the most vulnerable, we should recall Xenophon's advice about concern for the animal's mouth. The horse's mouth can become so toughened by prolonged use of a cruel bit that only an even crueler design will overcome increasing callousness and serve the intended purpose. There is a bit of no return.

Of all the devices used to break a

horse to the will of man, the harshness or gentleness of the bit sums up best a rider's attitude not only toward his horse but, by logical extension, toward all of nature. It symbolizes our desire to "master" our entire environment, regardless of the cost. The rider who makes regular and promiscuous use of a harsh bit is not aware that some of the best-behaved and most responsive horses have been trained with a hackamore—a bridle with reins and no bit at all. The result is the product of a gentle but firm education, not of brutality. Mastery is attained without cruelty.

The spur is a much later creation. It was known to the pre-Christian Celts, but was much "refined" during the Middle Ages and after—the period of the heavily-armored horse, when a rider's only way of touching the exposed flanks of the horse was with spurs.

The saddle seems to have been developed much more slowly and more

A MEDIEVAL ILLUMINATION OF A STRUGGLE BETWEEN A CRUSADER AND A SARACEN. (BRITISH MUSEUM)

61

casually than either bridle or bit. Since it was not so crucial a factor in controlling the horse, its evolution was more idiosyncratic, dependent on the need of the individual rider to accommodate his anatomy to the back of a horse. The saddle blanket was the first kind of upholstery that came between rider and horse. Luigi Gianoli, in *Horses and Horsemanship Through the Ages*, offers a plausible explanation of why so many centuries passed between the first use of the blanket and the general acceptance in western Europe of the saddle: "That delay does have an understandable motive. Try changing from an English saddle to a military one and then to a Western tree [saddle], and you will feel as if you had lost all contact with the horse, as well as the unpleasant suspicion that you cannot control his

actions. The same progression obtains in going from riding bareback to a saddle-cloth . . . and padded saddle."

The saddle proper, made with a framework of bone or metal and some sort of padding, is thought to have been first used widely in China during the Han Dynasty beginning about 200 B.C. A similar saddle was employed by the Romans of the first century A.D., and is believed to have been brought from central Asia by the earliest of the Asiatic "barbarians"—the Celts. Neither the Chinese nor Roman saddle was furnished with stirrups. As the role of the horse in war became more active, the saddle grew more complicated and heavier. It required an exceptionally secure seat to keep an armored rider firmly astride a mount during a jarring encounter with another horseman,

whether in a tournament joust or in real warfare.

When the broadsword and eventually the saber replaced battleaxe, mace, and lance as the principal weapons of the cavalryman, and when, as a result, the speed and agility of the horse became more important than his weight and brute strength, saddles were more lightly constructed once again, and their variety increased enormously. An amusing variation is the sidesaddle, thought to have evolved from the early packsaddle, a device not too different from the modern mulepack.

Just as it is probable that the earliest effective tamers of the horse were Brahmans, so it would seem that their Hindu descendants were the inventors of the stirrup. This gave the rider, and especially the rider who fought opponents

standing on firm ground, a stability on which he could depend. The first known stirrup, which dates to about the second century B.C., was designed to hold only the big toe of the rider, for the reason that the Indians did not wear boots or shoes. As horse-borne Hindu evangelists spread the teachings of Brahma across Asia to Korea and China, they carried with them the message of the stirrup. By the fifth century A.D., the boot-wearing Chinese used a stirrup similar to those of our own time. Presumably, the Turks got the word from the Chinese only after a battle in 694. Thus did Islam acquire knowledge of this invaluable accessory.

One authority asserts that the stirrup was the most significant development of warfare between the taming of the horse and the invention of gunpowder. Prior to its employment, the rider in battle always had to keep one hand on the pommel of his saddle or the mane of his horse. With his feet in stirrups, he could make use of both hands to wield his weapon and, equally important, he could use all the leverage afforded him by the weight of his torso. It augmented immensely his power on horseback. It was the stirrup that made possible subsequent refinements of armor.

WITH MAN
IN BATTLE

TO HORSE, YOU GALLANT PRINCES! STRAIGHT TO HORSE!
DO BUT BEHOLD YON POOR AND STARVED BAND
AND YOUR FAIR SHOW SHALL SUCK AWAY THEIR SOULS,
LEAVING THEM BUT THE SHALES AND HUSKS OF MEN.
HENRY V, SHAKESPEARE

The number of battles in which the cavalry charge proved the decisive element is literally in the thousands. Not even an entire volume devoted to the subject could give a comprehensive picture of this essential feature of war. Some battles, however, were particularly significant as turning points. We have already cited the exploits of Alexander the Great and his Bucephalus. His conquests, all largely attributable to clever management of cavalry, were crucial to the evolution of early western civilization. The successes achieved by the Romans on countless battlegrounds were ultimately as fateful, and it was the horse that not only made the long Pax Romana possible, but determined when Rome's influence began to decline —at Adrianopolis.

The early battles of the Christian era terminated with the most important, that of the Milvian Bridge in A.D. 312. This meeting between the troops of the western emperor, Maximus, and his rival from the east, Constantine, was decided in the latter's favor because the western Romans were not competent deployers of cavalry. Riding at the head of a large contingent of horsemen, Constantine carried the day, gaining control of Rome's empire in eastern Europe and Asia Minor. What remained in the west would eventually fall to the Goths. Constantine's triumph was so momentous, of course, because of his almost immediate conversion to the Christian faith. For the first time, all of civilized Europe had been made relatively safe for the defenders of the Church of Rome.

The only remarkable defeat of a superior cavalry force in the first Christian millennium was the victory of the Franks over the Moors at Poitiers in 732, discussed in the previous chapter. So astonishing was the outcome that the Christians ascribed it to divine intercession. The facts appear otherwise. Charles Martel, who commanded the Frankish force, had cavalry of his own,

though hardly to the number of 10,000, the estimated size of the Islamic army. He had, however, two advantages: a knowledge of the terrain and armor. He did not permit the enemy to determine how or where the battle was to be fought, and when the two forces came together, the armor worn by his riders and foot soldiers gave protection against the light weapons of the Moorish cavalry. Moreover, it seems that in any event this venture of Islam so far north into Europe was merely a maneuver intended to test the strength of the Christian defenses. It should also be noted that the Moslems retreated only to the northern slopes of the Pyrenees. It would be more than a half-century before Charlemagne drove them back into Spain.

During the Crusades, when Moor and Christian battled each other in their struggle to gain or regain a hold on the eastern Mediterranean shores, the forces of Genghis Khan, the Mongolian conqueror of thirteenth-century central Asia, were gathering in the east. Riding sturdy little horses that must have resembled the animals Captain Prjewalski discovered a hundred years ago, Genghis Khan's legions, after mastering their neighbors in what is now the Mongolian Republic of the Soviet Union, fanned out to the east and south. The Khan was an Asiatic Alexander. He had, like Saints Eloi and Dunstan, a reputation as a peerless smith. His grandson, Kublai Khan, together with his mounted warriors, would later prove quite as successful as the mighty Genghis.

Barely a half-century after the death of Genghis Khan, yet another empire was founded on horseback, this time by the Turkish conqueror Osman. His Ottomans, like the Mongolians, were horsemen of daring and skill, and it is testimony to the quality of their steeds that a Turkish stallion should be one of the first three horses to figure in the noble lineage of the Thoroughbred.

The advent of gunpowder in Europe did not for several centuries do much

PRECEDING PAGE: CAVALRY OFFICER CHARGING, *PROBABLY THE MOST CELEBRATED OF THE HORSE PICTURES BY THE 19TH– CENTURY FRENCH PAINTER, GÉRICAULT. (CLICHÉ DES MUSÉES NATIONAUX)*
ABOVE: THE TROJAN HORSE, *FROM A MEDIEVAL ILLUMINATED MANUSCRIPT. (BRITISH MUSEUM)*
OPPOSITE PAGE: IN A SCENE FROM *A RUSSIAN ILLUMINATED MANUSCRIPT, THE HORSE SEEMS TO PLAY THE SAME ROLE IN WAR AS HE DOES ELSEWHERE IN EUROPE AND ASIA. (BRITISH MUSEUM)*

71

BELOW: A DETAIL FROM NAPOLEON AT EYLAN BY ANTOINE JEAN GROS (CLICHÉ DES MUSÉES NATIONAUX)
RIGHT: THE BATTLE OF FLEURUS AS SHOWN ON AN 18TH–CENTURY SNUFFBOX LID. THE MOST ASTONISHING FEATURE OF THIS ENGAGEMENT IS THE USE OF A BALLOON FOR OBSERVATION. (IMPERIAL SCIENCE MUSEUM, LONDON)

to alter the use of cavalry. The explanation for this seems to be that artillery shot consisted at first of roundish stones and was notoriously inaccurate. In fact, a cannon was often more hazardous to those standing beside or behind its breach than those at whom its fire was aimed. Besides, a cannon required a minimum of two or even three minutes to load, fire, and reload—hardly an effective weapon against such rapidly moving targets as men on horseback.

The earliest effective use of the cannon was as a weapon of siege. Its fire could break down defensive walls and fortifications, allowing infantry and cavalry to penetrate enemy compounds. The development of field artillery increased the utility of the horse in warfare, for only horses (especially the great horse of the type that had carried armored knights in an earlier epoch) were strong enough to pull the enormous and cumbersome siege cannons and mortars.

Perhaps the other significant difference produced in war by the use of gunpowder, as far as the horse was concerned, was the sound of the explosion. An entire generation of war horses of all sorts must have been traumatized by the terrifying noise of the cannon and the arquebus. It added another element to the horse's ever more rigorous training for battle. But as he had earlier accustomed himself to other kinds of menace, the battle-horse dutifully learned his new lesson.

So cavalry remained a vital instrument of land warfare. Only in the eighteenth century were ordnance and powder sufficiently reliable to replace completely the bow, the pike, and the sword as weapons. Well into the nineteenth century, the role of cavalry remained significant. Although artillery

and musketry became increasingly accurate, the speed of the horse was still essential. One capacity alone made the light horse cavalry crucially useful—it could overrun enemy artillery batteries, thus preventing them from decimating infantry battalions.

The Battle of Omdurman, fought in the Sudan in 1898, is considered the last encounter in which cavalry troops, with sabers drawn, played a part worth mentioning in warfare. With explosives like nitroglycerin already in general use, and T.N.T. recently invented by Alfred Nobel, the days of the warhorse were numbered. At Omdurman, Kitchener's British horsemen carried pistols as well as swords, while their Mahdi opponents were armed mainly with spears.

But the fact that cavalry had finally lost its usefulness did not mean that units were immediately disbanded. There remained, even as recently as World War II, cavalry regiments in active service. However, the Poles would surely have made a better showing against the invading Nazis in 1939 had their troops been equipped with tanks and planes instead of horses.

Massed cavalry was only one aspect of the horse's importance in war. The

Washington at Princeton.
Fall of Gen'l Hugh Mercer.

mounted scout was invaluable. And draft animals were almost as helpful as the cavalry itself. Though it was the custom for armies to "live off the land" while on campaign, there were some supplies which could only be brought along by horse-drawn wagons. Vehicles were also required to carry off the spoils of war. Moreover, when an army was encamped in winter quarters in the field, the wagons were the only links with sources of supply. Later, when cannons and heavy mortars came into use, the draft horse assumed another vital role which he would retain until motorized artillery came into existence.

75

WITH MAN
AT WORK

*AWAY WITH THE CANT OF "MEASURES NOT MEN"!—THE IDLE
SUPPOSITION THAT IT IS THE HARNESS AND NOT THE HORSE
THAT DRAWS THE CHARIOT ALONG.
FROM A SPEECH GIVEN IN THE BRITISH
HOUSE OF COMMONS, 1801, BY GEORGE CANNING*

Although much of the text so far has been devoted to the role of the horse in battle, the creature's services have been more often devoted to the purposes of life and productive growth than to those of death and annihilation. It is, after all, man and not the horse who glorifies war and the instruments of destruction.

Even if the first harness known was designed for the use of oxen and applied only somewhat later to asses and onagers, we may be certain that some variety of harness was in use wherever the horse was available for work. The principal difference between the original harness and the contemporary one is the collar. Who invented that accessory, or whether it simply evolved like shoe and bridle and bit, is unknown. Nor are we sure to what peaceful use the harnessed horse was initially put.

It is possible that the two-wheeled cart or chariot was the first horse-drawn vehicle, and it is probable that it belonged to the rich—because horses were the rich man's prize. Egyptian relics suggest that in addition to the chariot's use in war, it was a means of transport for the great and a feature of the hunt. It was also used for racing. However, Greek and Roman enthusiasm for chariot-racing is better documented than that of Near Eastern civilizations.

The evolution of the harness is obscure because it was so rarely depicted by artists. If the horse did his job, that was all that counted. To have art objects showing horses at such lowly work as drawing a plow or pulling a cart seemed foolish. So it is only with the advent of sculptors, genre painters, and miniaturists of the Middle Ages and the Renaissance that details such as the harness were more or less systematically recorded.

It is instructive to consider how very long before the birth of Christ the harness was a practicable piece of equipment and how very little, from what we may now deduce, it has changed in four

or five millennia. True, leather and iron eventually replaced wood and cordage, but the basic operating theory of the harness has been surprisingly consistent since its invention. We do not know, however, the number of years or even centuries of trial and error preceding the discovery of the precise point on the horse's chest that could withstand the maximum pressure without seriously inhibiting natural motion or breathing.

Nor can we say how long it took for man to develop the horse's shafts and traces. Was it a mathematician or an artisan who first appreciated that the angle of the shafts had a direct bearing on the size of the load the horse could pull and the speed at which he could pull it? Though we cannot answer the question, we do know now that the angle of 12 degrees is optimal for the shafts of a racing sulky. Similarly, we are uncertain when the articulated four-wheeled vehicle was perfected. That invention was the key to the weight of the burden a horse could draw—in general, about six times the animal's own weight, taking into account the surface over which it was to be transported and the inclines and declines of the route.

But once such fundamentals had been mastered and a means of braking had been developed, modifications rather than dramatic changes occurred over

77

the centuries that followed. Agricultural implements disclose an identical pattern of evolution; pragmatic man did not alter basic designs that so admirably served their purposes.

Even in retrospect, not much glamor attaches to the horse and wagon, perhaps because there was not much glamor in daily life for the average human either. Whether the object drawn was a plow or a carriage, the work seemed drudgery for all concerned. There was a notable distinction, however, between the viewpoints of the driver and the horse when such drudgery was exacted. Man could think his way out of his predicament—or at least he was able to imagine such a possibility. The horse, once broken, adapted himself to whatever task, high or base, was assigned to him.

Though science knows more today than ever before about the temperament and psychology of the horse, it has yet to regard him as possessing a significant intellect. No dolphin he. Anthropomorphic literature, from *Doctor Doolittle* and *Black Beauty* to *My Friend Flicka*, never stretches even childish credulity in ascribing powers of reason

LEFT: *IN* FLATFORD MILL *(DETAIL), JOHN CONSTABLE, PROMINENT ENGLISH 18TH–CENTURY LANDSCAPIST, DEMONSTRATES HIS MASTERY OF THE PASTORAL SETTING. (TATE GALLERY, LONDON)*
TOP RIGHT: THE SAND TEAM, *A PAINTING OF A SCENE AT BIG SUR, IN CALIFORNIA, MADE EARLY IN THIS CENTURY BY GEORGE BELLOWS. (BROOKLYN MUSEUM, NEW YORK)*
BOTTOM RIGHT: THE INTERIOR OF A STABLE, *BY GEORGE MORLAND, A FAMOUS 18TH–CENTURY ENGLISH ARTIST BEST KNOWN FOR HIS HORSE SCENES. (THE TATE GALLERY, LONDON)*

to the horse. In such works, the animal is constantly surprised by the occurrences that befall him, and especially by the cruelty of man. The horse, as conceived by many writers, cannot project himself into a future, because to know that there is a future is to reason. Horses simply do not reason effectively. It is the present that preoccupies the horse, the need to survive. If working horses become restless, it is normally the result of prolonged confinement and inactivity. There is no insurrectionary horse—which is not to say that horses do not rebel against some kinds of savagery and servitude. But when they do, it is for reasons of self-preservation. It is, however, worth recalling again that everything man asks of the horse is against that creature's natural inclinations and instincts.

The atavism of the horse's genetic arrangements appears to be very powerful. Turn a horse loose to graze with a number of his fellows and he will soon revert to a stage closely resembling that of his earliest youth, before he was broken. If he is left for years or even months without human attention, he must be broken all over again before he can be put to use. That is why the few herds of horses that still roam the extensive ranges of the western United States are called "wild," though they are really feral. Psychologically, they very rapidly return to a state of absolute liberty, and physiologically they do so more and more with each succeeding generation in the wild. Allowed to roam freely and to breed without man's selective intervention, the horse reverts to something like his generic state with amazing speed.

Some of the earliest depictions of the horse at work are to be found in sculptured details of architecture and in the pottery and murals of Greece and Rome. Following the long epoch of the early Middle Ages and the onset of the Crusades, the horse once again is shown at his labors in the statuary that adorns Romanesque and early Gothic cathedrals and churches of western Europe, especially those of France, the Low Countries, and Germany. Illuminated manuscripts of the same era abound in illustrations of the draft horse at work. Here we observe the applications of horsepower in agriculture, in the construction of various kinds of buildings and fortifications, and in the transportation of goods and people—by cart, wagon, sledge, and sleigh. In the absence of navigable waterways, the horse provided the fastest and most reliable means of communication. The postal systems of

all Eurasia depended on the horse wherever sea or inland watercourses were not available.

Well into the eighteenth century, horses remained the prerequisites of wealth and rank, the peasantry and urban poor having barely enough to house and feed themselves. Even assuming that a poor man could get himself a horse, he could not afford to care for it or equip it for riding or driving. The lower classes did, however, look after their masters' animals, and in many instances were more skilled than the owners in training, handling, and nurturing them. Indeed, there was an affinity between the ostler and the horse; they shared an equally enforceable fealty to the same proprietor, and stablehands may have felt a stronger bond with the working breeds than with the more temperamental animals reserved for war, sport, and ceremony. One thing is certain: the order of things operated to the benefit of the horse, not to the man who took care of him. It was easier by far to replace a good ostler than to find another well-trained, well-bred horse.

Wider distribution of horse-ownership was closely associated with the rise of the middle class—the merchants and bankers and professionals who became increasingly important to the

economy of western European countries following the earliest of the Crusades and during the Renaissance. To this period we can trace the increasing popularity of the cob—the ordinary, gentle-mannered and amiable saddle horse which would carry even the unskilled rider without much danger of shying, bolting, or taking the bit between his teeth and running away with his passenger.

Even in the eighteenth century, use of the horse in the civilian life of Europe was restricted mainly to the propertied classes of town and country, or to those who had to ride because of their employment by the propertied classes. Such was also principally true of "public" transport—the diligence or stagecoach—reserved for travelers who could pay the comparatively high fares. Besides, until the eighteenth century and its industrial revolution, the poor had little occasion for journeys they could not manage on foot.

In only one aspect of European life throughout the Renaissance, the Reformation, and the eighteenth century was the horse in the possession of the poor: The mountebanks and charlatans and quacks, the players and acrobats of traveling shows, were carried from town to town in fancifully decorated vehicles drawn by gaudily caparisoned horses. In this case alone, static bondage was replaced, for a handful of souls, by precarious vagabondage.

Well into the nineteenth century, the horse, like the most arable land, was still owned mostly by the rich. But there were

OPPOSITE: PONY AND CART IN NEW YORK'S CENTRAL PARK EARLY IN THE PRESENT CENTURY. (CULVER PICTURES)
BELOW: OF ALL THE PEACEFUL USES OF THE DRAFTHORSE, THAT OF PULLING FIRE APPARATUS WAS SURELY ONE OF THE MOST IMPORTANT. (WIDE WORLD PHOTOS)

increasing exceptions. In countries where great holdings had been broken up by revolution, as in France and the United States, the yeoman farmer and the merchant each owned at least one horse whose purpose was utilitarian. But one had to look to the New World to discover a lower class that could afford to own horses.

The working horse was never assigned a more demanding or prolonged task than the one presented him in the Americas. The horse carried the white men as they subdued two continents, depriving the natives first of their lands and ultimately of their freedom. Later, horses served to control the ever-growing herds of cattle that ranged about the immense, fenceless ranches of the New World. Later still, as the population of the United States moved westward, the horse and the ox pulled the famous Conestoga wagons.

The Pony Express was perhaps the most spectacular peaceful use to which the horse was ever put in the New World. Enduring barely eighteen months, from the spring of 1860 to the autumn of 1861, this enterprise contracted to carry letters from Saint Joseph, Missouri, to Sacramento, California—a distance of more than 1,800 miles—in ten days. Remount stations were located along the route at intervals of from 7 to 20 miles, each rider covering about 75 miles before handing on his special *mochila* (a stoutly-made leather mail pouch) to his relief. The horses employed for this brief experiment in communications were principally Quarter horses. Rarely did the mail reach its destination in the prescribed time; there were many factors to contend with—hostile Indians, washed-out trails, and in the terrible western

winter, snow-covered passes. The Pony Express was a financial failure and was rendered unnecessary by the completion of a telegraph line to the Pacific coast in October of 1861.

Everywhere else in the world, as in the Western Hemisphere, the horse was the most important means of conveyance for those who upheld law and order by a system of drumhead justice. Even in such refinements of man's inhumanity to man as torture and execution, the horse was assigned a role. Four horses were the source of power used for drawing and quartering a victim convicted of a great crime against the state in England and elsewhere. And in the New World, he frequently bore the victim of lynching. The rider's neck was tied to the branch of a tree by a rope. At a given moment, the horse was whipped, causing him to lurch forward, leaving the rider suspended in air. Indeed, there was hardly an aspect of human life or death in which the horse failed to share.

OPPOSITE: GYPSY CARAVANS, A SCENE PAINTED IN SOUTHERN FRANCE BY THE FAMOUS FRENCH POST-IMPRESSIONIST, VINCENT VAN GOGH. (CLICHÉ DES MUSÉES NATIONAUX)
BELOW: A HORSE-DRAWN WAGON AT BAKU, NEAR THE CASPIAN SEA. (CULVER PICTURES)

RETURN TO THE NEW WORLD

*[THE NATIVES] HAD NEVER SEEN HORSES UP TO THIS TIME
AND THOUGHT THE HORSE AND RIDER WERE ALL ONE ANIMAL.*
TRUE HISTORY OF THE CONQUEST OF NEW SPAIN,
BERNAL DIAZ DEL CASTILLO

As we have observed, the horse had long been extinct in the Western Hemisphere. The effect that the absence of domesticated beasts of burden had on the development of North and South American cultures can best be measured by a comparison of the growth and interaction of the cultures of Eurasia and North Africa. There is no reason to suppose, for example, that the Aztec, Mayan, and Incan civilizations were inherently less open to cultivation than their counterparts abroad. What hindered their growth and dissemination was an almost complete lack of intercultural exchange, and this defect could be ascribed principally to the lack of reliable long-distance land transportation—i.e., the horse, camel, or dromedary. The llama proved an inadequate substitute, and in Arctic regions of North America, the musk ox has been tamed only in recent years.

Everything was abruptly and appallingly altered by the arrival in the New World of the European. According to the biography of Christopher Columbus by his son, the great explorer brought with him on his second westward voyage a number of mares and stallions. These he landed on the island of Hispaniola (now the Dominican Republic and Haiti), the original Spanish colony of the hemisphere. It is interesting to note that among the thousands of islands of the Caribbean, several were later selected as ideal for the breeding of horses—especially Jamaica and Cuba. The natives were quick to understand the utility of the strange creature. In these earliest of New World stud-farm undertakings, the native inhabitants were aided and instructed by the Spanish invaders.

The arrival of the horse by water, as noted before, was already a part of Old World mythologies. However, to transport horses over wide stretches of uncharted seas was far more difficult than the Mediterranean adventures of the

past—for the horse as well as man. It was probably rendered more hazardous by the perplexing patterns of the winds that prevailed on the last leg of the voyage from Europe or Africa. Some historians have conjectured that it was during this earliest of westward explorations that the seas bounded by 30° of latitude north and south of the equator acquired the name of "Horse Latitudes." Whether or not this is so, the barometric highs that typify the Horse Latitudes produce long periods of windlessness. On a voyage through this area, as many as half the horses languishing in a ship's stuffy hold would perish from thirst and tropical heat. In exactly the same way, later on, African slaves succumbed by the thousands. There was a difference, however. At the journey's end, the surviving horses enjoyed a happier fate, for the most part, than the surviving slaves.

Of the bloodstock brought from Spain to the New World we shall have more to say in a later chapter. The Spanish horse was remotely descended from the famed Arab mares which had crossed the Strait of Gibraltar to bring Islam to Europe in the eighth century. Wherever the Spaniards ventured in their explorations of North as well as Central and South America, they brought their horses, and they always lost a few. This attrition was not always due to death or injury. The natives saw nothing wrong in a bit of thievery. The aliens were raping and plundering; why should their victims not reciprocate as best they could—by stealing horses whenever the opportunity presented itself?

In his *True History of the Conquest of New Spain*, Bernal Diáz del Castillo, himself a participant in that venture, recounted the events of Cortés' first encounter with the Mexican natives in

89

ABOVE: BRONCO BUSTER, *A BRONZE STATUETTE BY FREDERIC REMINGTON, ONE OF THE MOST FAMOUS ARTISTS OF THE WEST. (PHILBROOK ART CENTER, TULSA)*
OPPOSITE: *THE CHEYENNE INDIANS DEMONSTRATED ON PAINTED AND QUILLED BUFFALO HIDES THE IMPORTANCE OF THE HORSE IN THEIR LIVES AND RITUALS. (DENVER ART MUSEUM)*

1519. The Spaniards easily prevailed in this skirmish. Diáz inscribed one sentence, however, which abruptly takes us back three millennia: "[The natives] had never seen horses up to this time and thought the horse and rider were all one animal." So was the legend of the centaur re-enacted in the New World.

Not until the end of the sixteenth century did the "Indians" of the Americas acquire horses in numbers that were militarily useful—that is, sufficient to allow them to think themselves capable of driving the white man back into the Gulf of Mexico. The reason for this great lapse of time was bluntly set forth by Diáz: "Horses and blacks were worth their weight in gold." The African blacks were at this time used mainly on the islands of the Caribbean; the Indians of the mainland provided plentiful slave labor there. But the precious horses were jealously protected.

Nevertheless, as cattle were introduced to graze on the lush, virgin grasslands of Mexico and Florida, the natives, of necessity, became cowboys—*vaqueros*. Although the law imposed by the Spaniards forbade the conquered people to own horses and permitted them to ride only with their masters' explicit approval, the Indians became familiar with the creatures' habits, and they learned, more or less, how to care for them.

Not before 1598, when the Spanish Juan de Oñate settled the land which is now a portion of Texas bordering on the Rio Grande did the Indians of the Southwest become equestrians in significant numbers. Only then did the invading white men discover themselves occasionally at the mercy of the people whom they had enslaved.

The first tribe to acquire and master

horses in what is now the southwestern United States was the Apache nation. By the end of the seventeenth century, the Apaches were redoubtable horsemen, elusive because they were normally migratory—followers of the buffalo—and because the horse gave them far greater mobility than they had ever before enjoyed. Inspired by the Apaches, other Indian nations rose against the Spanish in 1680. The so-called Pueblo revolt which began in that year was the signal for a general slaughter of whites that would eventually (but only temporarily) restore to the natives their hold on the southwest part of North America. This task could not possibly have been managed without the horse. All that Indians required to give them full parity with the whites was the gun. They had understandable difficulty securing arms and ammunition from their enemies in

Mexico, but they found in the French traders and missionaries and the few British who had traveled so far south and west a willing source. It seemed to the governments of Paris and London sound policy to check Spanish colonization. If this could be achieved by arming the Indians, so much the better. Had the Apaches and their allies known of the experience of Indians of the Northeast and the Atlantic seaboard, they might have wondered whether the bargain was as good as it seemed.

With respect to the horses purloined from the Spanish, a curious process immediately set in. Skilled riders and husbanders though they were, the red men of the Southwest knew nothing of the breeding techniques developed in the Old World. This ignorance, probably coupled with a severe want of suitable diet and the custom of allowing their

herds of horses to graze and mate at will, occasioned a devolution among all their animals. The Indian horse of the Southwest became feral. To the degree that these horses were allowed to roam, feed, and breed indiscriminately, they reverted to a state like that of true wildness. The effect of this on the appearance and physical condition of these horses was startling. They became smaller, the shape of their heads became more angular and less refined than those of their Arabian forebears. Increasingly did these "mustangs" resemble some of the primordial strains.

TYPICAL VEHICLES OF 19TH-CENTURY AMERICA. BOTTOM: ROAD WAGON, DOUBLE HARNESS. (CULVER PICTURES)
TOP OF PAGE, LEFT TO RIGHT: DETAIL OF CLOSED CARRIAGE FROM CITY HALL, NEW YORK, 1824, BY TOBIAS
YOUNG; WOODCART, MILKWOMAN, AND MAN WITH UMBRELLA ON DRAY, BY AUGUST KÖLLNER; DETAIL FROM
TRINITY CHURCH, NEW YORK, 1824, BY TOBIAS YOUNG. (FRICK ART REFERENCE LIBRARY, NEW YORK)

FOR MAN'S AMUSEMENT

There was no single moment or period when the horse ceased to be solely utilitarian and became a source simply of man's amusement, any more than there was a date when the chase was no longer necessary to man's survival and became at least partially a sport. The change from one to the other was gradual wherever and whenever it occurred. It depended on the development of agriculture and animal husbandry in any particular civilization, as well as on the leisure available to the sportsman. We cannot even be positive that hunting was the first sporting use of the horse's speed and agility, though this seems probable.

It is likely that the chase enjoyed a long transitional phase when it was simultaneously necessity and sport. The same was almost surely true of horse racing—though again we are confronted with difficulty in ascertaining place and era of origin. Can there be any doubt, given man's competitive instinct and urge to gamble, that two or more proto-historic horsemen wagered a day's game or a stag's antlers that one mount was faster-paced than another? The beginnings of formal racing, however, with reasonably fair starts and finishes, was probably the invention of some Near Eastern potentate who had horses to spare for this kind of diversion.

Whether chariot-racing preceded the ancient equivalent of modern flat-racing we cannot say. It is possible, despite the fact that no pictorial representations of the sport survive. The Hittite cuneiform manual of horse care suggests that the flat race flourished in the middle of the second millennium B.C. Moreover, polo was played by the cavalrymen of Darius at the time that Alexander the Great overpowered the Persian Empire. If men were playing polo in the fourth century B.C., they were bound to be testing the speed of their horses on the flat. But of these challenges we do not have graphic evidence.

96

Scenes in sculpture and murals and on pottery from these pre-Christian days are devoted to the racing of chariots. The record abounds in examples from all civilizations that bordered the eastern Mediterranean. The beginnings of organized flat-racing, on the other hand, are not so well documented.

The distinction between a cavalry charge and a point-to-point race must, at the outset, have been merely a matter of the object of the exercise. The cavalry charge gave birth to the steeplechase; of that much we may be pretty sure, if we take into account the essence of any society's foreign policy: to preserve itself from invasion and, as a corollary, to invade the territory of its neighbors. As noted, the role of the horse in conquest was vital, and an important measure of any cavalry's effectiveness was its speed.

The earliest racing of chariots is better recorded than other equine competitions, because it required some sort of arena, track, or course. Only towns and cities could afford such elaborate facilities. To construct and maintain a surface large enough to accommodate two or more chariots side by side was within the capabilities only of the rich— be they rulers, aristocrats, or generals. Similarly, only great men and their entertainments were thought worthy of memorializing in art.

Racing on the backs of horses, however, made no such demands of the terrain. It may well have begun on arid stretches of desert or plain. Until the organization of the Olympic games— the original ones, that is—this sort of competition was mainly informal, whether cross-country passages or on the thoroughfares of towns. We know, however, from Plutarch's account, that

Philip of Macedonia rejoiced to learn that on a single day his son Alexander was born, his army had defeated the Illyrians, and one of his stallions had won a race at Olympia. By Philip's day, two Greeks, Simon of Athens and Xenophon, had contributed useful advice for competition riders. By then, too, the Persians enjoyed racing on the flat as well as polo. In both instances, it is likely that these tests of speed took place on courses originally laid out for the racing of chariots. Of the Persian races we have no pictorial evidence, but the Greeks and Romans have left us many.

From Ancient Roman Amusements to the Tournament

The Romans assimilated from the various cultures they vanquished much that was known about the horse, both as an instrument of work and of diversion, military or civil. Not until our own day would harness racing be as popular as it was in the cities of the Italian peninsula during the long summer of Roman civilization. The Romans imported stallions and mares from all the regions of their enormous empire for breeding and cross-breeding. Thus were they able to produce strains of horses to suit every need. Their theories and techniques were very sophisticated, even when appraised by the scientific standards of today. Although most of these breeding arts were lost with the onset of the Middle Ages, we are able to reconstruct from surviving documents the development of hunters, short-distance and long-haul draft horses, an ambler whose gait must have closely resembled that of the Tennessee Walking horse, the great horse of the Gauls which, as the Ardennes, carried the armored knights of a later epoch, a trotter, a parade horse, a war horse, and

100

—naturally—a racehorse. Breeders of the past two centuries have refined the methods used by the Romans, but it is nonetheless remarkable that these ancients were able to develop so wide a range of types.

It is a symptom of the disease which, we are often told, led to the fall of Rome that the late Romans were so proficient in the fields of sports and entertainment. They tended increasingly to leave the waging of war to mercenaries; this applied as much to cavalry as to infantry. It was a mark of gentility to be a skilled equestrian, and there were schools of horsemanship in many cities of Latium where young men of fortunate birth could learn to ride—but only for amusement and for the good impression it would make on others, not for use in war.

In contrast, the racing chariots that were a craze of the principal Italian towns were driven almost exclusively by professionals. The owners of the animals and vehicles were unwilling to risk their own necks in these chariot contests, won by hook or crook. Horses were frequently drugged, injured, or intimidated. Drivers were bribed, chariots were sabotaged. These activities were quite against the rules, of course, but great sums were waged on the outcome of the races, and the rules were constantly broken. It is difficult today to imagine the frenzy of a chariot race in ancient Rome. The Circus Maximus was the empire's largest track, providing a surface a bit less than three furlongs in circumference. It was wide enough to accommodate the ten-horse teams which were the ultimate racing machines of the fourth and early fifth centuries. Immense crowds, comprising all elements of the populace, came to these events.

102

The charioteers of this period were probably more renowned than their modern counterparts of the harness and motor tracks, and the best of them became, relatively, as prosperous. They earned every dinar; for in addition to the risks of the actual race, there were hazards before the contests were under way. The emperor Caracalla murdered one charioteer who was scheduled to drive a team which would oppose his own. The sinister emperor Caligula was guilty of a similar offense. Nor were such crimes confined to the rulers of Rome. The most celebrated drivers had bodyguards and food-tasters who protected them against assault and poison—as if, indeed, they were themselves emperors.

With the decline of Rome and the coming of the barbarian hordes, sport abruptly entered a period of obscurity. There was simply no time for the kind of entertainment with which the rich and poor of the empire had diverted themselves when they should have been minding the marches and forming cavalry ranks. However, the later Middle Ages witnessed the birth of the rituals and formalities of the tournament. This was a logical feature of knighthood and chivalry stimulated by the Crusades. Though it was a vastly more savage discipline for man and horse than the niceties of dressage and courtly equitation and the controlled leaps of stadium jumping and cross-country riding, the medieval and Renaissance tourney clearly foreshadowed the modern horse show and Olympic events.

The legends, traditions, and literature of the tournament were a great deal more glamorous and romantic than those of our present-day Olympic competitions. For they included, in addition

ABOVE: TOURNAMENT ON THE GROUNDS OF A CHATEAU, *BY THE FLEMISH MASTER RUBENS, SHOWS HIS OWN COUNTRY HOUSE. (CLICHÉ DES MUSÉES NATIONAUX)*
TOP LEFT: THE JOUST OF SAINT INGILBERT, *AN ILLUSTRATION FROM FROISSANT'S* CHRONICLES, *AN EARLY FRENCH HISTORICAL WORK. (BRITISH MUSEUM)*
BOTTOM LEFT: ONE OF THE FIRST BRITISH ART PATRONS, SIR GEOFFREY LUTTRELL, RECEIVES HIS HELMET FROM HIS WIFE, AS SHOWN IN AN ILLUMINATION FROM A MEDIEVAL PSALTER. (BRITISH MUSEUM)*

POLO, AS SHOWN IN A PHOTOGRAPH OF A GAME
BETWEEN FLORIDA AND CUBAN TEAMS, DEMANDS
GREAT STAMINA AND AGILITY OF BOTH HORSE AND
RIDER. (UNITED PRESS INTERNATIONAL)

to skill and speed, overtones of religion, quest for personal glory, and not a little sexuality. In order to qualify as a knight, an aspirant had first to prove himself as an athlete, a good hand with horses, and a competent servant of his lord. He certainly had no need for book-learning. He did not even have to be literate. However, he did have to demonstrate his religious devotion and it was not unusual for him to join one of the holy military orders, such as the Knights Templar or the Knights of Saint John. It was the custom, too, once he had been received as a knight, for the youthful *chevalier* to select as his patroness a lady of impeccable virtue, sometimes the Virgin herself.

The "sports" of the tourney, as practiced by the knights and lords with savagery, cunning, and recklessness, were also games of war. But they had so much in their favor as entertainment that they long outlived their relevance to war as it was eventually waged. By the early years of the seventeenth century, the tournament had become empty ceremony for knights and barons who had been left behind by history, and for ladies often the subject of poems that made very light of their virtue. Because the language of chivalry is traditionally French, the myth has persisted that gallantry and nobility were mainly Gallic. However, the heroes of the tourney came from all parts of the western world.

Polo

Of sports that are performed on the backs of horses but are not directly connected with the chase or with war, polo is surely the oldest. The name of the game in English derives, it is thought, from the Tibetan word for ball, *pulu*, though the sport itself long antedates this name. As noted before, a form of polo was played by the Persian and Bactrian cavalrymen when Alexander defeated Darius, but the rules and practices of the game they took part in are unknown. It is strange that the Greeks were not sufficiently attracted by the sport to bring it home with them. Whatever the reason, polo did not make its way westward at this time, but did gradually spread north and south and, eventually, east—to Byzantium, Turkestan, India, China, and Japan. For more than 2,000 years after the death of Alexander, polo was a game restricted to the Near and Far East.

In 1859, polo captured the imagination of the British masters of India, near Manipur. The next year, there was a British-sponsored polo club at Calcutta. A decade later, the game was imported for the amusement of the pleasure-loving aristocracy of Britain. The organization of play was not, apparently, based on the personal experience of the hussars who participated in the sport in India, but rather on written descriptions sent back to London from Calcutta.

In 1871, there was a formal polo match between members of two British cavalry regiments. Each team at this time consisted of eight members; two years afterward, the number was reduced to five, and in 1882, to four. By the end of the nineteenth century, polo was securely established in Britain and on the Continent, with rules of play very much as they are today. By 1886, the game had spread to the United States, where it was only significantly modified by the handicapping of players for all but international matches. While handicapping can scarcely be said to have brought polo within the reach of the masses, it had the virtue of placing inept players more or less on a level with their betters.

Polo today has suffered important setbacks, especially in the eastern United States. The problems besetting it are several, all financial in one way or another. To reserve only for polo a field 300 yards long is difficult in areas where the value of real estate is constantly soar-

ing. To stable and care for a string of polo ponies (never less than a dozen for a single team, and preferably sixteen) demands considerable monetary resources. And, finally, polo has just never been a sport that attracts large crowds.

Nevertheless, in some sections of the American Midwest and far West, polo continues to flourish politely. It is a game of great attraction to the informed spectator—rather like soccer on horseback. There are hazards involved for both mount and rider. The long, flexible-handled mallet can easily injure—which is why the players wear special helmets and the horses' forelegs are protected with padding. But we are not likely to see in the immediate future a serious revival of interest in polo.

Bullfighting

Of all the sports in which the horse has a role to play, bullfighting is by all odds the cruelest insofar as the fate of the mount is concerned. Even the joust and other aspects of the medieval tournament were fairer, for the horse was a genuine member of the team; he shared the danger with his rider. In bullfighting, he is the pitiable pawn, although some effort has been made in recent years to ameliorate the conditions for horses.

Horses in bullfighting are ridden by *picadores* whose purpose is to goad the bull into the rage required to make him a suitable opponent for the *torero*, the bullfighter. The means by which this is accomplished are simple enough. The *picador* rides his usually ancient and

106

spavined steed close enough to the bull to taunt him. The horse, under the circumstances, is not overeager to approach the young animal, but is wary of his horns and strength, uncertain of his own footing and ability to escape. The horse is usually given blinkers, and often an actual blindfold over one eye, to prevent him from seeing the creature he is pitted against. In addition, a padded leather apron affords some measure of safety, provided the bull charges with his horns held high enough. However, it is frequently the case that the bull, holding his forehead almost parallel with the ground, brings his horns into contact with the unprotected belly of the horse. The result, alas, is not instant death, but a prolonged agony in which the horse's entrails are torn out as the bull removes his horns. The horse expires terribly, and is drawn from the arena by a team of donkeys.

The ignoble role imposed on the horse is rarely dwelt on in literature. The reason for this lacuna is obvious: those who love the pageantry and color of the sport tend to ignore its unpleasantness; even those who deplore its cruelty tend to concentrate their attention on the unequal struggle between man and bull. The hapless horse is usually overlooked, despite some contemporary attempts to offer him additional protections. Even Goya, one of the most honest of all pictorial annalists of the *corrida*, depicted only rarely the ignominy reserved for the horse.

Bullfighting, along lines now considered "classic," is a Spanish modification of a pastime imported to Iberia by the invading Moors. As practiced by them, it was a diversion nasty only for the bulls. The Spaniards refined it, adding the *picador* and, of course, his pathetic

A COWGIRL BEING THROWN FROM A BRONCO. (CULVER PICTURES)

mount. They could see no good reason for committing useful horses to so obscene an end.

Goya has brilliantly recorded, in a series of etchings, the evolution in his native Spain of the *corrida*. On several occasions in that country and in other Spanish-influenced lands, as well as in France (where a less sanguinary version of the amusement is very popular), bullfighting has been suppressed on moral grounds, but always its attraction has proved so great that politicians have found it expedient to legalize it again.

The Rodeo

One of the most spectacular of modern entertainments involving the horse is the rodeo, an American diversion which evolved informally in the western part of the country in the two decades before the Civil War. Because so many of the words connected with this celebration of horsemanship are Spanish in origin, it is usually assumed that the techniques were developed in Texas while that vast territory was still, at least technically, a possession of Mexico. The word "rodeo" is a corruption of *rodear*, to encircle. "Bronco," "lasso," "lariat," and "mustang" are likewise derived from the Spanish *broncho*, *lazo*, *riata*, and *mesteno*.

The early rodeos were events organized in western cowtowns after roundup time, when *vaqueros*, the cowhands, had money to spend on wagers and drink and only each other to amuse. Although no specific record remains of any of these occurrences, they are so firmly fixed in the folklore of the early Southwest that there is no doubt of how or why they took place. The difference of opinion which, as Mark Twain wrote, makes for horse races also made for rodeos. Their first features were probably flat races over short distances to demonstrate the speed of the mustangs and/or Quarter horses that were the usual mounts of the cowboy. Other feats must soon have been added—bronco-riding, roping of steers, and eventually demonstrations of riding tricks—as the years passed and the West's population grew.

The first rodeo of record in which cowhands from more than one ranch took part occurred in 1869 at Deer Trail, Colorado, where teams from three spreads participated. Far more ambitious events, involving representatives from a far greater number of ranches, took place over the next twelve or thirteen years in towns as remote from each other as Cheyenne, Wyoming, and Winfield, Kansas. To Pecos, Texas, goes the honor of being the first to sponsor a rodeo in which cash prizes were offered to the winners of each event. Four years later, at Denver, spectators were charged admission for the first time—and the age of rodeo as we now know it had begun.

The difference between the rodeo and other equine competitions lies mainly in the fact that—originally, at any rate —it was a demonstration of the crafts of the working cowhand and his working horse. (An exception is the pulling contest staged by teams of draft horses that is still a feature of some Midwestern fairs.) Even the bronco-busting, today a "staged" affair in which the horse is induced to buck by the application of a bucking-strap, was at first a proof of a cowboy's ability to subdue an unbroken horse or one that had previously failed to respond to precisely this crude method of mastering animals. The latter variety of horse was treasured in somewhat the same way that especially aggressive bulls for the *corrida* are reserved for the most audacious *toreros*.

THE RODEO PROVIDES THE QUARTER HORSE AND HIS RIDER WITH MANY OPPORTUNITIES TO SHOW THEIR REMARKABLE COORDINATION, AS IN THIS EXHIBITION OF CALFROPING. (UNITED PRESS INTERNATIONAL)

It was in 1897 that the first of the major rodeos of a style we can recognize today was presented at Cheyenne. Others of similar character were organized at Pendleton, Oregon, at Calgary, Alberta, and at Salinas, California. From these developed the circuit which has today expanded to include the larger indoor and outdoor arenas of virtually every major American city—the greatest of all being the December National Finals in Los Angeles. The Rodeo Cowboys Association, the organization that is the authority for the sport, recognizes more than 600 different rodeos throughout the country in which prizes amounting to more than $4 million are awarded each year. From every point of view it is big business, attracting about twelve million spectators annually—a figure surpassing the attendance of either of the major baseball leagues.

Rodeo events have increased considerably in number and variety since their early days. They have something to please (and perhaps offend) almost everyone—including races of various kinds, bareback and other trick riding demonstrations and/or contests, roping, bulldogging (wrestling steers to the ground), riding of bulls and broncos. In addition, there are "novelty" features —a kind of slalom racing with barrels as obstacles, and inevitably, clown-riders.

Unlike the feats of the primitive rodeos, those of the modern events are usually made "against the clock." For example, an official success for a bareback ride of a bronco lasts only eight seconds. To make his ride count, the rider must stay atop a saddled bronco for two seconds longer. The advantage of a saddle over bareback is more apparent than real, however, since the stirrups may prove as much a hazard as an asset,

110

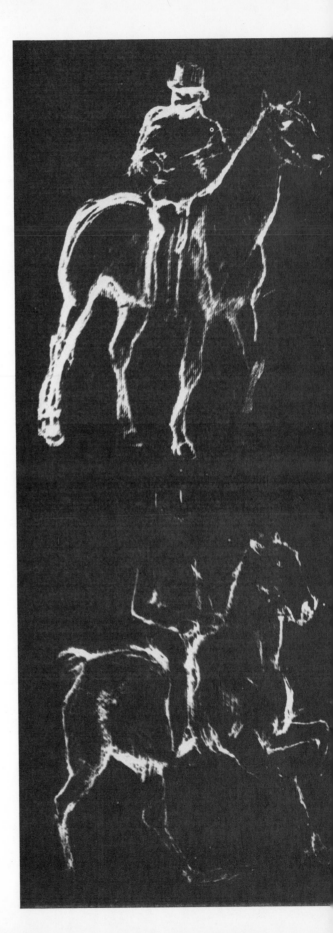

and although the pommel or "horn" of the saddle is there to be grasped, the rider who does it—who "pulls leather"—is disqualified.

As in the appraisal of Olympic competition, provision is also made for "style"—the savagery of the horse and the audacity of the rider. It is obligatory in both bareback and saddled contests for the horse to be spurred at least once as it emerges from the chute; ideally, it should be spurred as often as the rider can manage for the duration of the ride. Assuming that the cowboy has been able to remain on the mount for the requisite time, he is removed by a pickup rider. More often than not, the contestant finds himself sprawled on the ground before the time limit has elapsed. It is a tough way to make a living. Judging both bareback and saddled events is predicated on a maximum score of 100, awarded by two judges, each of whom is allotted 25 points for the performance of the rider, 25 for that of the horse.

Quite different and much more demonstrative of the dexterity of the horse and the horsemanship of the cowboy is the exhibition of calf-roping. Although time is also a factor of major importance, it is the skill of the teamed man and horse that counts the most here. The horse must have attributes of instant start and stop and turn so that the rider may judge the direction and speed of the 400-pound calf, rope him neatly, and bring him to the ground in what seems a single flowing motion, binding the animal's legs in such a way that, after he removes his hands from the rope, the knot holds for a minimum of five seconds.

Steer wrestling, or bulldogging, involves a rider and an assistant, the "hazer," whose task it is to ride along one

OVERLEAF: SIGHTS AT THE FAIR GROUND, *A CURRIER & IVES PRINT, SHOWS AT ONCE THE FESTIVITY AND PRACTICAL ASPECTS OF AN AMERICAN COUNTRY FAIR IN THE LAST CENTURY, WHERE ANIMALS WERE SHOWN AND TRADED. (METROPOLITAN MUSEUM OF ART, GIFT OF MISS A. COLGATE)*

side of the steer to prevent him from veering away from a straight course. Although the horse employed for this sport must have speed, it is not necessary that he be endowed with the virtues of the roping horse, since what is basically required of him is that he be able to propel his rider in such a way that at just the right moment he may leap from the saddle and grasp the steer's horns and neck, literally wrestling him to the ground. Of course, time is of the essence here as well.

The final "classic" rodeo event is bull riding. The requirements and features of this exploit are fundamentally the same as for bareback riding. The rider must stay on the back of an unhappy bull for eight seconds, with nothing more to cling to than a rope loosely tied about the animal's midsection.

Horse Shows and Horsemanship

The development of the horse show is basically the result of the military, civil, and hunting uses of the horse. The earliest of such formal displays were offered purely for the enjoyment of the Austro-Hungarian imperial court in Vienna. However, both before and after the Spanish Riding School was founded, there were town and village fairs where horses were put up for sale or barter and made to go through their paces. Out of these casually organized gatherings the most celebrated of horse shows evolved and eventually became regular events in Europe and the Americas.

Undoubtedly the greatest variety of classes is offered by horse shows in the United States because they must reflect the extraordinary diversity of interest shown by American breeders, trainers, and exhibitors. A simple listing of the categories recognized by the American

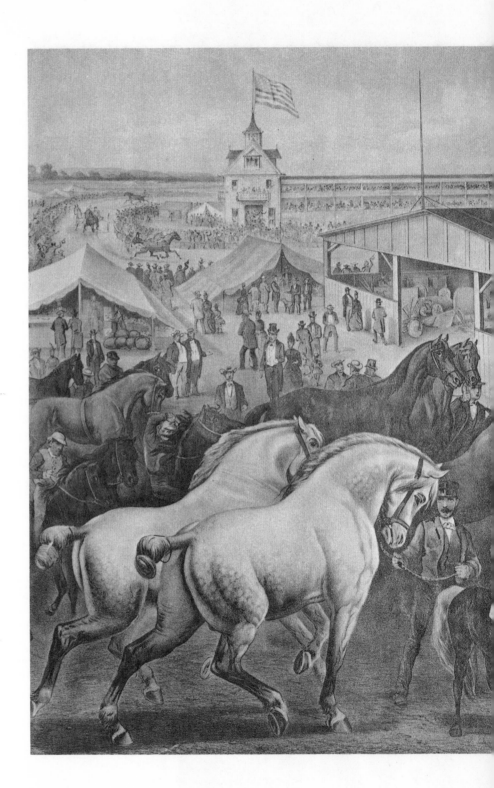

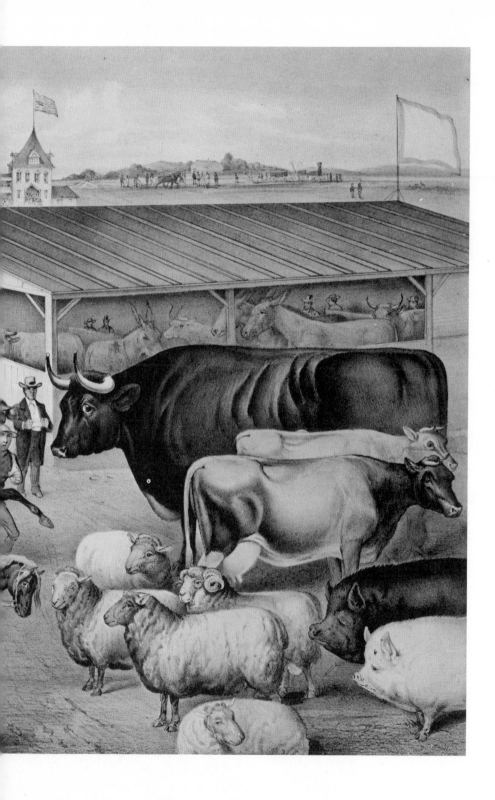

Horse Shows Association, principal authority of shows in the United States, will give the reader an idea of the scope possible for any accredited event: Arabian, Combined Training (three-day event), Dressage, Equitation (in three kinds of competition riding), Hackney, Harness, Hunter, Jumper, Junior, Morgan, Palomino, Parade horse, Polo pony, Roadster, Saddle horse, Shetland pony, Walking horse, Welsh pony, and Western horse. It should be added at once that not every horse show, and not even every great one, offers classes in each of these categories, but if the demand exists, it can be accommodated.

Wherever there is a major horse show, it is usually the focus of considerable social attention. The opening of New York's National Horse Show, for instance, is considered so important a social event that it attracts in gala evening dress a vast number of individuals whose interest in horses is far less consuming than their concern to be seen in the right place at the right time. So it is in other American and European cities. Horse Show Week in Dublin comes in early August, when it is literally impossible to find a hotel vacancy within miles of the horse show grounds.

Although a discussion of each kind of horse that takes part in a horse show is reserved for the following chapter, in which the breeds are described, there is one aspect of horse show competition that is not associated with any particular kind of horse. This is horsemanship. Antoine d'Aure, one of the major French authorities on the subject, wrote that "Breaking a horse to obedience, appropriating his means to our necessities, conserving and developing the qualities inherent in him . . . comprise the art of equitation."

ABOVE: THE CIRCUS, BY GEORGES SEURAT, A POST-
IMPRESSIONIST PAINTER, SHOWS THE HORSE IN A CLASSIC
ROLE AS ENTERTAINER. (CLICHÉ DES MUSÉES NATIONAUX)
BOTTOM, FAR RIGHT: A TRAINER CAUSES A LIPIZZANER TO
BOW. THIS MOVEMENT MAY BE AN ADAPTATION OF THE
ARAB CUSTOM OF MAKING A CAMEL KNEEL TO FACILITATE
MOUNTING. (UNITED PRESS INTERNATIONAL)

114

FROM ITS INCEPTION, THE CIRCUS WAS A
SHOWCASE FOR TRICK HORSES AND RIDERS,
AS IS EVIDENT IN THESE FOUR CIRCUS
PICTURES OF THE NINETEENTH CENTURY.
(CULVER PICTURES)

A HAPPY BOY AND HIS PONY, AFTER WINNING FIRST PRIZE IN A COUNTRY SHOW EVENT. (BUDD STUDIOS, NEW YORK)

We shall not try to trace here the history of theories of horsemanship. The illustrations in this book are adequate commentaries on the changing styles of riding. Since the time of the Greeks, man has been writing about how a horse ought to be ridden. As a rule, the abundant literature, much of it by cavalrymen for cavalrymen, has concerned itself with mastery of the animal—that is, domination. It was only at the very end of the nineteenth century that Federico Caprilli revolutionized military and eventually popular equestrian thinking about the management of the mount. Caprilli, who fell from a horse and died in 1907, would never know that he had developed his principles just in time for them not much longer to be of serious military value. The use of cavalry soon came to an end. But his theories were nevertheless adopted by almost every army before 1914.

The essence of Caprilli's message was startling in its simplicity. Although motion pictures had some time earlier demonstrated precisely how a horse moved at every gait, the Italian seems to have been the first riding instructor of importance to make a study of this motion and to note, as a result, how earlier styles of equitation tended to inhibit the animal's freedom of action, especially when jumping. It is to Caprilli that we owe the conception of the forward seat, which requires that when the horse is on the point of leaving the ground, the rider must rise a few inches from the saddle, incline his torso quite markedly forward, allowing the reins to slacken so that the horse may extend its neck in a manner which, as Caprilli had remarked when watching animals training on a *longe* (a long rope or strap), is perfectly natural to it.

If we compare the forward-seat rider with those reactionaries (most of them British and many of them steeplechase jockeys) who persist in leaning backward as the horse goes over an obstacle, we are astonished that it required so many centuries for man to make so obvious a discovery. Why some riders continue to follow the ancient way is perplexing. Jockeys insist that the short stirrup they use causes them to lose control of their horses. Others make much the same assertion, without the excuse of having to ride short. One may find some justification in the argument of the jockeys, none for the others.

We do not know whether Caprilli had an opportunity to view slow-motion studies of the horse in action. But we do know that until these films were generally available, even the most knowledgeable horse people refused to believe that all four of the animal's feet left the ground simultaneously at the gallop—though a careful consideration of footprint patterns ought to have offered them conclusive evidence of this truth.

Caprilli, like many other geniuses, was extremely dogmatic. He said, for example, "The two types of equitation, for show and for the field, are, in my view, contrary to one another, and mutually exclusive or destructive." By this he seemed to suggest that the demands of the show ring—specifically, dressage events—inhibited the free-flowing motion required of the cavalry horse. The immediate result of this dictum was the abolition of dressage practice in the Italian cavalry. However, riders of the three-day event continue to demonstrate that Caprilli was wrong in this particular conclusion. There were many Caprillian die-hards. When, as a boy of twelve, I suggested to my own instructor (who was a Russian disciple of Caprilli) that the master seemed to be in error on this point, I had my ears boxed—literally. And later, when I won some important dressage and jumping events on the same horse, I lost that splenetic gentleman's friendship for life, for I had menaced his blind acceptance of Caprilli's absolute wisdom.

Disputes are not confined to theory. Consider the saddle and bridle, the martingale, the use of blinkers . . . but mostly, consider the saddle. As a matter of pure prejudice, I have never ridden a western saddle (which has a horn in front). I once sat on a United States cavalry saddle, a type of western saddle, and dismounted abruptly, convinced that I should be immediately unmanned by its peculiar contours, even at a gentle gait. I have heard renowned riders from the American West describe the English saddle as "effete," presumably because, like the bikini, there isn't much to it. Obviously, we are both in error. Each piece of tack, like each style of riding, is an adaptation to a need. Only a fool would ride a western saddle in a jumping competition. Only a fool would attempt to rope a steer while riding an English saddle. So it is with horsemanship. In the horseman's house there are many mansions.

While horsemanship is, in various degrees, an ingredient of practically all modern applications of the horse in sport and entertainment, it is particularly stressed in the activities of such groups as the Pony Clubs, the equine activities of 4-H Clubs, and even in apparently casual diversions like trail riding. If the rider is not able to manage a horse, the experience is unsafe at any speed.

The Circus

Comparatively little serious scholarship has so far been devoted to the horse as merely an entertainment. For one thing, the line between the "trick" horse and the animal that is simply very well trained—the school or dressage horse—is not always easy to draw. The circus horse has been a staple of traveling shows from the moment the modern circus came into being in Britain in the late eighteenth century. It is said that Philip Astley, a retired sergeant-major who had served in a regiment of cavalry conscripted from the class of shopkeepers and tradesmen (and consequently referred to derisively as the "regiment of tailors"), offered in 1770 the first display that more or less conforms to our present notions of the circus. Setting himself up on a plot of land near Westminster Bridge in London, he not only dazzled crowds with exhibitions of trick riding but is believed also to have pro-

vided his audiences with the first "comedy" ride—a commentary on the "regiment of tailors" which had, despite its nickname, proved a valiant troop. Astley's most daring display was to stand on the back of a horse as it cantered in a circle.

Trick riding and tricks performed by horses have made some forward strides since then, but most of them are only modest variations—so far as the horse is concerned, refinements chiefly in degree. For once a horse has been disciplined to the point where he can perform one difficult stunt, it is only a matter of time and patience before he can be trained to do others.

Riding appears to have been the central feature of the circuses in America that began to capture the public imagination in 1785, when Thomas Poole installed himself at Boston, New York, and Philadelphia. In each town he spent several weeks in every season, alternatively giving exhibitions of fearless trick riding and furnishing instruction in horsemanship to eager pupils. The long and colorful evolution of the circus since that day has invariably included at least one act in which the horse is a principal attraction. A poster of 1891 advertising the Barnum and Bailey show proclaims: "The most accomplished & dauntless lady riders in a spirited & dashing *original* HURDLE RACE, with free rein bravely & fearlessly taking the most difficult leaps & dangerous obstacles." All kinds of acrobatics were accomplished on the backs of tranquil, steady horses—and still are. The horse, moreover, is frequently starred in circus features, sometimes in a dignified if gaudy manner, sometimes as clown.

Without seeking to belittle the accomplishments of the circus horse or the

A FAMOUS MOVIE HORSE, TRIGGER, IMPRESSES HIS FOOTPRINT ON THE SIDEWALK OF GRAUMANN'S CHINESE THEATER IN HOLLYWOOD AS HIS OWNERS, FILM STARS ROY ROGERS AND DALE EVANS, LOOK ON. (CULVER PICTURES)

OPPOSITE PAGE: A SEQUENCE SHOWING THE NORMAL WALKING GAIT OF A HORSE, TAKEN BY EADWEARD MUYBRIDGE, PIONEER OF CINEMATOGRAPHY. (AMERICAN MUSEUM OF NATURAL HISTORY)

  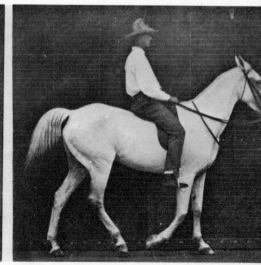

skills of the circus rider, we must observe that the typical flummery of the circus performance is to the high-school performance what the early airplane is to the space vehicle. *Haute école* equitation, as practiced by the experts, is ballet in the strictest classical sense.

The Movies

No book devoted to the horse would be complete without at least a passing reference to his contribution to the motion picture. It should be noted that the first step in the development of cinematography was a multiple-camera study of the movements of the horse made jointly by Eadweard Muybridge and his assistant, John Isaacs. Muybridge's ingenious though cumbersome equipment made possible stop-action photographs that demonstrated conclusively that, for instance, at canter and gallop all of the horse's feet leave the ground at once.

The role of the horse in the long history of the film is striking. The most popular and least destructible mode, the western, would of course be inconceivable without the horse. During the heyday of the staple "horse opera," the mount was probably as important to the success and popularity of the work as the rider.

Although *The Great Train Robbery*, made in 1903, is commonly thought to be the first of the western movies, it appears that as early as 1898 all the ingredients that have since become the most beloved clichés of the genre were evident in a short feature made for the Edison Company: *Cripple Creek Barroom*. But it was undoubtedly *The Great Train Robbery* that established for millions of viewers the charms of excitement and knowing anticipation that have made the western film so durable a form of entertainment.

Only five years elapsed before the emergence of a star—Broncho Billy Anderson—whose first venture, made in 1908, was *Broncho Billy and the Baby*, a short which rejoiced in such popular acclaim that during the ensuing seven years no less than 500 successors, of one- or two-reel length, were put together. Although the Anderson films definitely established the prime importance of a strongman personality as the hero whose reactions to given conditions were as predictable as those of good infielders managing a double play, the similar impact of the horse was yet to be made.

The first of the "great" stars of the standard western epic, William S. Hart, made one remembered effort to give the star treatment to a horse (named Fritz). Indeed, Fritz had a second distinction—that of being used as leverage in a quarrel between Hart and his producer, Thomas H. Ince. When the star broke with Ince, he saw to it that Fritz, a "personality" animal, was no longer used in films made by the producer.

Hart's successor as king of the horse opera was Tom Mix, who seems not to have made a fetish of any particular horse. The same cannot be said, of course, for the "Lone Ranger," whose mount, Silver, was part of his cry as he and Tonto rode out to preserve virtue or restore justice. Two other horses that became stars in their own right were Champion and Trigger, the respective mounts of Gene Autry and Roy Rogers. Trigger was billed as "the smartest horse in the world," a claim no one has been in a position to dispute.

In developing the personalities of "personality" horses, one consideration is the age of the animal. As will be noted later in discussing the length of time required to train a Lipizzaner, as many as seven years may be needed to bring an animal to his peak. With stars as durable as Autry and Rogers, it was surely necessary to create doubles for their horses —both for purposes of performing tricks that were unduly hazardous to a horse of the star category and to succeed the original in the event of injury or death or decrepitude. In photographs of Champion taken at different times, it is possible to detect differences in the blaze of the horse's face, leading one inescapably to the conclusion that there were at least two "Champions." The procedure is known informally as "ringing," which is the subject of a selection in the Appendix.

Horses trained for cinematic use are closely akin to those employed in circuses. The degree of schooling is just as great in teaching a horse to stumble and

120

FLAT RACING, THE SPORT OF
KINGS, IS THE ULTIMATE TEST
OF THE THOROUGHBRED. HERE,
AT AQUEDUCT, ONE OF NEW
YORK CITY'S TWO MAJOR FLAT-
RACING COURSES, MOUNTS
MAKE THEIR DASH FOR THE
FINISH. (WALTER OSBORNE)

fall on command as to rear, to wheel, or to sidestep. And to the rider, a fall may be even more dangerous.

The movie horse is a creature embedded in the folklore of the twentieth century wherever films are shown. He had his apotheosis, perhaps, in *Cat Ballou*, a film that was somewhat disrespectful of certain western clichés. At a critical moment, the horse and his rider, Lee Marvin, are propped against a wall. Marvin, nursing a severe hangover, is barely conscious. The horse, his legs crazily crossed, looks spavined and near collapse—hardly the pair likely to save the heroine from death on the gallows. Nevertheless, when the crisis is upon them, they rise to the occasion in such a way that even Bellerophon and Pegasus might envy them.

Dressage and the Three-day Event

The terms "dressage," "combined training," and "three-day event," which we have frequently used in this book, embody a good part of what has already been said about equitation and management of the horse. The creature that performs in the three-day event is subjected to combined training, of which dressage is an essential part. The three-day event is surely the apogee of horsemanship, for in each of its aspects it demands different and extremely difficult talents of both horse and rider —dexterity, agility, good temper, enormous stamina, and a considerable amount of plain brute strength.

If you plan to compete for a place on your country's Olympic equestrian team, you will certainly have begun to ride seriously long before you read this book. You will have been given manuals and elaborate charts. You will probably have read most of the popular works mentioned in the chapter about the horse in literature. You will have studied photographs and slow-motion films of this most strenuous of all the events in which any horse today participates. You will be fairly inundated by statistical data of every sort. A stopwatch will be constantly operating in your head. There is no more rigorous training for horse and rider than that which precedes competition in the Olympic three-day event, or in any of the preliminary elimination contests. If they can perform even moderately well in that arduous activity, they will perform admirably in any other equestrian exercise that they attempt.

As earlier remarked, the three-day event evolved from the training of the cavalry horse. It became a feature of the Olympics at Stockholm in 1912, when teams from eleven countries competed. But it was only after the games of 1920 that the present, highly organized event was devised. It has been a phenomenon of the era following World War II that non-military participants have been in the majority among three-day-event competitors.

There are three Olympic equestrian competitions, of which the three-day event constitutes only one—though it incorporates features of the other two, and more. These are the *grand prix du dressage* and jumping. In addition to these contests, the three-day event includes a cross-country passage which is a test of all the equine and equestrian virtues not tried in the other two competitions—notably poise and endurance of both mount and rider when confronted by difficult terrain and unfamiliar obstacles.

Time is a vital element in all aspects of the three-day event. The dressage por-

BRONCO RIDING IS ONE OF THE MOST POPULAR AND SPECTACULAR FEATURES OF THE RODEO. RIDERS NEED TO REMAIN MOUNTED FOR ONLY A FEW SECONDS, BUT FEW SUCCEED. (WALTER OSBORNE)

tion, which occupies the first day, is closely comparable to the schools portion of Olympic figure skating competitions. That is, the exercises to be performed are absolutely stylized. It is a sport for the entertainment only of spectators who know precisely what each pairing of horse and rider is expected to accomplish. In the opinion of those who are addicted to it, dressage is the most consummate manifestation of horsemanship in that it requires of the mount and his master a harmony so subtle that it is practically imperceptible. If a rider is seen or heard to coax his

horse, he will lose precious points. To the uninitiated, dressage has the appearance of a rather simpleminded game. For, after all, what the horse does is to spend something between 7½ and 15 minutes in an arena (dimensions, usually 20 by 60 meters), during which time he stands, walks, backs up, trots, and canters. The variations of this drill are the "manner" in which these gaits are executed—natural, collected, and extended. These maneuvers must be executed in different portions of the arena— these denoted by large letters placed along the edges. The horse may be asked

to leap a low obstacle—not to demonstrate his jumping talent, but rather his style and that of the rider. That, in fact, is all there really is to dressage, but such a description is comparable to the observation that *Hamlet* is a play about a man who is unable to make up his mind.

The emphasis in dressage is on the precision of the horse's movements, the degree of control exercised by the rider, and something common to many other Olympic events—"style." Anyone who has not personally attempted dressage is almost sure to find watching an exhibition of it a great bore. It is somewhat like watching ballet dancers practicing at the *barre* for hours on end. Yet this is the almost secret appeal of dressage. It is very much "inside stuff." The audience for it is the smallest of any of the three parts of the three-day event in international competition.

All the same, dressage gains annually in popularity—partly because more and more spectators understand it, partly because of what the word itself (borrowed from the French, like most of its terms) means in English: training. The rider who genuinely masters dressage is

127

able, by extension, to master all other aspects of riding with relative ease, for the rider and horse are perfectly attuned to each other.

The specific exercises and routes to be executed in a dressage performance are described in a diagram furnished to each contestant, who is well advised to memorize them before entering the dressage ring for his individual showing. Using the letters on the arena's borders as guides, the rider takes his mount through a series of prescribed routines at the three gaits, including a canter in which the horse is expected to change leads when making turns and even to canter placing the incorrect foot forward merely to demonstrate the animal's submission to his master's will. Three basic patterns are followed—the figure eight, the serpentine, and the circle, all of whose dimensions are denoted by the guide letters. In addition, the mount must perform certain other movements —pirouette, pivot, passage, piaffer, shoulder-in, travers, renvers, and transversal. These are rather specialized and showy maneuvers designed, as is all dressage, to prove the control of rider over horse. It is important to remember that the entire dressage exhibition asks of the creature nothing that is not natural to him; the movements called for are those that a supple, sensitive horse is not only able to do but in fact *does* on occasion without command—like the piaffer, for instance, which is a little trot in place. Dressage has been rightly compared to calisthenics, muscular and disciplinary tune-ups for rider as well as mount. Lest the aspiring rider be discouraged by the demands of the dressage ring, he should recall that in many local horse shows there are several classes of dressage, ranging in difficulty from "A"

through "D." Class D, however, is not the ultimate stage; *that* is the *haute école* exhibition, which will be described in the section devoted to the Lipizzaner horse made famous by the Spanish Riding School of Vienna.

The most physically demanding aspect of the three-day event is the cross-country ride and steeplechase competition on the second day. Since the distance and difficulty of the course vary markedly from place to place, the only constant is the stamina of the horse and rider. It is an exercise which is not easy to observe, for it covers a large area—usually a distance of about 16 miles. It is like trying to follow an automobile rally on foot. Although the speed at which a rider covers the course is a significant factor in the score he accumulates, there are also demerits for a horse's refusal to take an obstacle, for a rider's fall, as well as for failing to complete the course within the prescribed period. Riders are started individually at intervals, so that their race is more against the clock than against one another.

The third portion of the three-day event, show or stadium jumping, is the one most familiar to spectators. Though the obstacles provided may be no more than 4 feet in height—child's play for the competent hunter or jumper—it must be remembered that the horses which participate in this exhibition are the same ones that took part in the dressage demonstration of the first day and the cross-country section of the second. To say the entries in the three-day event are well-rounded competitors, horses and riders alike, is an understatement. Pairs that survive the second day's grueling test, not to mention the veterinary examination prior to their admission to the competition of the final day, have to be admired for even having reached this point.

The horse that can endure so severe a trial of physique and dexterity is extremely exceptional. Most of the animals entered successfully in three-day events are crossbreeds of various combinations. An Anglo-Norman, ridden by a French officer, was the 1968 Olympic champion. The rider, too, is a rather rare being, for he or she must become totally at one with the mount, to the point where—to bring us back almost to the beginning of this book—the rider and the horse are, in effect, a single creature, like the centaurs of mythology. It has been said of the horse suitable for the event that he must have abject confidence in his rider —so much so that he would, if asked, leap off a roof on command, certain that his master would never ask of him what he is incapable of accomplishing. A three-day event rider of my acquaintance has described the relationship between herself and her horse as a *folie à deux*—like marriage.

AT THE SUMMER OLYMPICS IN MUNICH, 1972, A MEMBER OF THE UNITED STATES EQUESTRIAN TEAM TAKES HIS HORSE OVER A RAIL FENCE. (PHOTO: PATRICK LYNCH)

HORSES OF EVERY KIND

*IN THE CHOICE OF A HORSE AND A WIFE, A MAN MUST PLEASE
HIMSELF, IGNORING THE OPINION AND ADVICE OF FRIENDS.
RIDING RECOLLECTIONS, G. J. WHYTE-MELVILLE*

Daphne Machin Goodall, whose photographic study, *Horses of the World*, is very nearly definitive, distinguishes and illustrates more than three hundred breeds of horse and pony. Her classifications are broken down not merely by continent, but often by nation, and occasionally by region or locality. Useful as this approach is for scholars, the truth is that today most breeds, whatever their origin, are found everywhere. Since the majority of them are bred on almost every continent, it may be more helpful to treat this topic in terms of types than of breeds; a great many breeds are the result of a bewildering succession of crosses and a staggeringly complex ancestry.

All contemporary horses are descendants of one of the primordial strains of *equus*. Dr. George Gaylord Simpson, a leading American authority, alludes in a major work, *Horses*, to a theory of equine genetics which he neither wholly accepts or rejects. A similarly equivocal

position is taken by R. S. Summerhays, a famous British scholar, in his *Encyclopedia for Horsemen*. This hypothesis sets up a rather sharp distinction between "hot-blood" (or "warm-blood") and "cold-blood" horses. The difference, it should be added at once, has nothing to do with the animal's normal body temperature, but concerns the climate and terrain in which a breed's ancestors evolved. Dr. Simpson, incidentally, recognizes no more than sixty breeds.

Stated a little more concisely than is strictly accurate, the theory is this: The "cold-blood" horse originated in the northern regions of the Old World, where the atmosphere was typified by sharp extremes of chill and warmth and where the pasturage available was usually lush and plentiful. The antecedents of the "warm-blood" horse, to the contrary, were found in hotter, more arid areas, where the grazing was sparser and water at a premium. The "cold-blood" type is deemed the more tract-

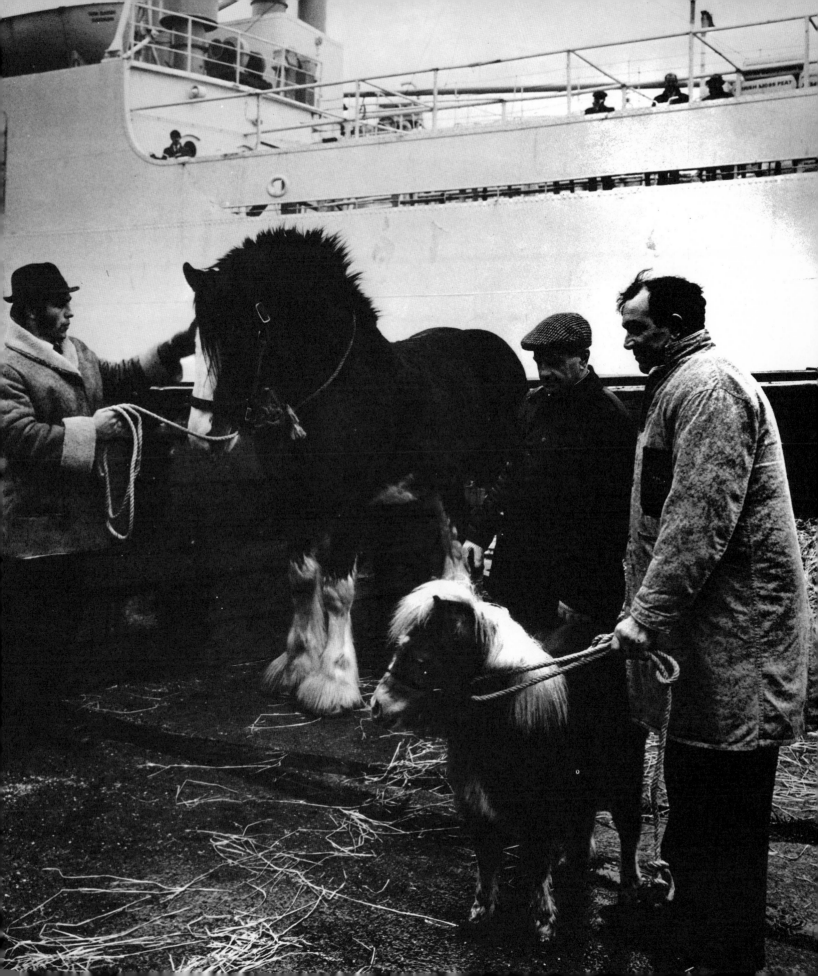

able of the two varieties because his progenitors had no need, as it were, to struggle for survival in the way the "warm-bloods" did. The latter is considered more alert, more mettlesome, and endowed with greater stamina.

The "cold-bloods" in their original condition may not always have been very tall, but as a classification they were heavier and more powerful than the "warm-bloods." The archetypal "cold-blood" is the Ardennes of Belgium and France, almost certainly the descendant of the great horse that bore the weight of armored knights during the middle ages, the horse that carried Gaul to victory before the Roman conquest. Although these massive, tall, and enormously strong creatures are comparatively numerous in their varieties, they represent only a handful when juxtaposed with the array of "warm-blood" breeds and the crossbreeds.

Differences of size, temperament, speed, stamina, and muscularity are, as we have observed, in large part attributable (according to the blood theory)

to climate and normal grazing conditions. But in our own era, such geographic distinctions apply essentially to horses that are allowed to run absolutely free. Great horses, Shetland ponies, and Argentinian miniature horses survive in this century as distinct entities only because of the most scrupulous breeding practices.

The "warm-blood" horses are those endowed with admixtures of Turk, Arab, or Barb in their lineage, creatures that were all conditioned in ancient days to endure in hot, dry, poorly-vegetated territory. From these high-strung animals are derived the fast-paced Thoroughbred, the Standardbred, the steeplechaser, the hunter, the three-day-event horse, the Lipizzaner, the hackney, the Morgan, the carriage horse, the Quarter horse, the cob, the polo pony, the Palomino, and the Appaloosa—indeed, virtually every all-purpose horse we recognize.

Splendid conformation in a horse, like "beauty" in an object of art, reposes essentially in the eye of the beholder. For this reason, breeders have propounded objective standards which, in effect, define equine beauty; subjective judgment has been all but eliminated, at least in theory. A quality Thoroughbred is not supposed to resemble a Shetland pony. A Quarter horse is not supposed to look like a Clydesdale. However, *all* horses and ponies have the same number of bones and teeth and muscles. The differences are in size and mass.

Before coming to a description and history of some of the major breeds of horse and pony, it may be wise to offer some observations about the horse, *per se*. All that has been discussed so far has related to the horse's evolution in

132

SAINT MARTIN AND THE BEGGAR,
*PAINTED BY EL GRECO DURING
THE ARTIST'S LONG STAY IN
TOLEDO, DEMONSTRATES THE
CURIOUS ELONGATION OF FIGURES
THAT MARKS HIS STYLE.
(NATIONAL GALLERY OF ART,
WIDENER COLLECTION)*

MONGOL CIRCUS, *A SILK SCROLL PAINTING AFTER*
CHAO YUNG, ILLUSTRATES THE ROLE OF THE HORSE
IN ENTERTAINMENT IN 14TH–CENTURY CHINA.
(DETAIL, METROPOLITAN MUSEUM OF ART, GIFT
OF A. W. BAHR)

TO CARRY MAN UPON HIS BACK IS ONE OF THE HORSE'S
MOST FREQUENT TASKS. SHOWN HERE IS A SADDLE HORSE
FROM A ROYAL MOGUL STABLE. (METROPOLITAN MUSEUM
OF ART, FLETCHER FUND)

history and his use in life. But to his individual structure and growth we have made reference only in passing.

The first thing one must bear in mind when coming into contact with a horse is that he is not a dog. The truism may appear frivolous, but one need only recall the majority of writings, films, and television programs devoted to this wonderful animal to realize that insofar as the horse is a central figure in such works, he is treated as prodigious. But there are very few prodigious horses in actuality. The prodigies of real life have demonstrated such qualities only after long and often harsh schooling.

So it is essential to understand the psychological nature of the horse. We have already frequently remarked that he is a creature of the herd. Each herd, as our observations of the surviving wild and feral animals indicate, has a stallion for leader. Except for a small number of younger stallions which make occasional and rather timorous efforts to displace this chief, obedience to the herd instinct is pretty nearly absolute. The horse is easily panicked. His impulses are governed primarily by a fear for his personal safety; and, as many cross-country riders will testify, it doesn't take very much to cause a nervy horse to shy. He is a terrific xenophobe. A close friend of mine occupied the better part of two full days and evenings trying to persuade an ancient mare to

LEFT: AN APPALOOSA, ONE OF THE BREED CREATED BY THE NEZ PERCÉS INDIANS FOR HUNTING AND PULLING LOADS, IS LED IN THE WILDERNESS COUNTRY OF THE AMERICAN WEST. (WALTER OSBORNE)

ON A FLORIDA RANCH, THOROUGHBRED COLTS AND FILLIES FOLLOW THEIR MOTHERS, TRUE TO THE HERD INSTINCT. (UNITED PRESS INTERNATIONAL)

enter a trailer. The horse was reluctant not because she had had a bad experience in a trailer, but because she had had no experience at all in a trailer. The solution was to show that it was perfectly safe by walking another horse into the vehicle. The old mare then went in without a murmur or gesture of protest.

This apprehension about the unknown explains, for instance, why many apparently courageous and very valuable racehorses and steeplechasers are provided with companions, especially when traveling. Of a more docile temperament than the high-strung beasts, these stablemates—sometimes not horses, but donkeys, goats, cats, or dogs—calm the precious creatures by giving them a feeling of familiarity, whatever the novelty of the surroundings in which they find themselves. When Thoroughbreds and steeplechasers are introduced for the first time to the electric starting gate, they must frequently be blindfolded, so alarmed are they at being even briefly confined to a padded cubicle. In the British Isles, where the electric gate was first employed only a few years ago, the horse regarded it as a revolutionary invention, one that few Thoroughbreds welcomed.

A contemplation of the horse in his more or less natural state is instructive in other ways. From the moment of his birth, almost literally, the foal can see and walk. Within an hour or so of his delivery, he is able to run with the herd. After he has been weaned, a gradual process normally completed within a few months, he begins to feed exactly as his elders do. Like the bovines, the horse is a grazer; but unlike breeds of cattle, the horse is not a ruminant. It is his habit to eat a little all the time. If he is given a large quantity of food in a single portion, his remarkably small stomach will become distended and he will suffer an extremely painful indigestion, colic, a condition that can become greatly aggravated if he has access to water after having so gorged himself. That is why domesticated horses are usually allowed only limited quantities of water and, as a rule, before their meals; the fluids, which they utilize as slowly as they do solid nourishment, accelerate the digestive process. The colic which results from overfeeding (or from too rapid feeding) is potentially a serious complaint because the horse is not physiologically equipped to regurgitate gases or excesses of feed.

The timidity which is part of the herd syndrome should yield the trainer some useful information in matters of handling, especially during the earliest phases of the animal's introduction to servitude. We have made the point that horses do not retain genetically from one generation to the next the inclination to domestication. Each foal must be bent to the will of its tamer as were its mother and father before it. But each foal does retain, indeed, often most "unreasonably," habit patterns based on its very first experience at the hands of man.

This does not mean, alas, that a gentle early education will invariably make for a gentle horse. Moreover, if one plans to train a horse to perform certain unnatural acts, it is likely that the patient but firm instruction solemnly and properly advocated by humane societies all over the world will fail. The technique required to induce a horse to perform anything like true prodigies is that of the carrot and the stick—with a much heavier emphasis on the stick. It is fear, as we have noted in connection with the training of cavalry and tournament and "trick" horses, that persuades a creature to do things that do not naturally appeal to him. He may quite understandably not be very eager to leap over a five-foot wall, for example. (Frederico Tesio, an Italian theorist, gave it as his opinion that horses are not, by natural instinct, jumpers at all. Turn a horse loose in a fenced field, he wrote, and he will make no effort as a rule to escape by leaping over the barrier, though freedom may seem to lie on the other side of it.)

To cite another instance, it is not the horse's normal custom to canter gently about a circle while an agile human leaps on and off his back. The rack and the single foot and the amble are not gaits with which the horse is born. Steeplechasing horses are not naturally suicidal, nor do they even fall down, except by accident. Their limbs are easily sprained or broken if the fall is an awkward one. Consequently, every time a cayuse in a western movie bites the dust, remember that he is doing so on sternest command. The force behind that command is a fear measurably greater than the fear of being injured from the fall, a fear which the horse understands from experience. It is possible that he will not be hurt when, on his master's command, he falls. He is *sure* that he will be punished severely if he refuses to fall. The carrot proffered for making a good fall is not so great as the apprehension generated by failure. There is no need to dwell here on the unattractive but comparatively efficient methods employed by professional trainers to make horses perform all kinds of exceptional and unnatural movements—prodigies.

However, the training of a horse for services in man's pleasure in what we think of as natural ways (we think them so because we have been compelling the horse to do these things for so many millennia) involves the same judicious application of carrot and stick used by the trainer of the prodigious horse. The difference is simply one of degree. It is a question of coercion. The horse does not want to do anything but graze with his fellow creatures, fly from his natural enemies, and reproduce his kind. Those elementary desires are common in equal measure to the Thoroughbred, the Mustang, and the Siberian wild horse.

It is true, of course, that the Thoroughbred and other refined varieties of horse have, over the centuries of their evolution under human aegis, developed characteristics which adapt a particular breed to certain kinds of work. Size, bone structure, conformation, and natural spirit endow given types with the physical capacity and will to carry out specific sorts of tasks. However, capacity and instinct are not synonymous. It is through coercion (which we dignify by calling it schooling or training) that a horse learns to combine his capacity and instinct in ways that man regards as useful to him. It is the horse's instinct to know his way back to his stable because that is where his food and his place of repose are situated. It is man who knows how to persuade him to run in an exactly opposite direction.

Lest we permit ourselves to become oversentimental about the plight of the horse, we should stay in touch with the comforting reality that most horses today are kindly reared and gently trained —for the very good pecuniary reason that in an era when the creature has lost virtually all of his practical utility, the demands imposed on him require his submission to few terrible or traumatic ordeals. He is no longer asked to take his

master to the wars or to pull impossible loads under appalling conditions, and rarely is he required to labor himself to death. It is a commonplace to observe that men treat horses better in this century than they treat many of their fellow men.

Because the horse has been for so many millennia a vital feature of comfortable human existence, more nonsense has been written about his physiology and psychology than about those of any other animals, except ourselves. During the long period between the death of Xenophon and the Renaissance, a body of horse lore, empirical but with large additions of magic and witchcraft, developed in much the same way that medical science grew. Xenophon's wisdom was not very widely disseminated. Not many people who had to deal regularly with horses were able to read, and even those who successfully absorbed his lessons learned very little about the horse in what we would describe as scientific terms.

Yet a surprising amount of the conventional wisdom about the horse, cherished for a couple of thousand years before the beginning of modern veterinary science in the last century, was accurate. If contemporaries no longer write, as did Shakespeare in *The Taming of the Shrew*, of the bots and the fives, the glanders and lampass, they do still refer gravely to such arcane complaints as forelegs that are tied in or camped, of heads that are hared or muttoned, of quittar, laminitis, thrush, ringbone, shoe boil, curb, mud fever, bog spavin, and windgall.

To a people that has reached the moon, it comes as a gloomy revelation to appreciate how very little, modern science notwithstanding, we know today about the ills to which horseflesh is heir. The catastrophic epidemic of equine encephalitis that caused the death or destruction of thousands of horses in the summer and autumn of 1971 throughout the southwestern portions of North America is only one major instance of this ignorance.

A substantial number of modern nostrums can, for all the miracles of modern veterinary science, be traced back to the Middle Ages—when it was sometimes more important to save the life of a horse than that of a man. Saint Eloi's insufferable arrogance was firmly founded upon that very reality; a skilled farrier was the most valuable servant of any cavalry. With cavalry came power. And power, as James Stephens observed in that Irish masterpiece, *The Crock of Gold*, "is man's secret." And for many thousands of years, no power was more important to man than horsepower.

Here, then, are some descriptions of the kinds of horse that man developed over those years.

The Heavy Draft Horse

The great "cold-blood" horse of antique days was, as we have already observed, a denizen of the temperate zones where pasturage was abundant and rich. This phenomenon explains the proliferation of these creatures in northwestern continental Europe and on the islands of Great Britain and Ireland. It appears that this original great horse was the forebear of the Ardennes or Belgian and that, in turn, all other animals of such stature have been developed from the Ardennes. Standing about 16 hands, he was not usually "great" in height. It is only when we compare him, for example, with the Arab or little *equus caballus prjewalskii* that we discern

important skeletal and muscular distinctions which resulted from climatic and geographic conditions in which he evolved during prehistoric times.

In almost every northern European country there are variants of the great draft horse, many of them larger and stronger than the Ardennes: the French Percheron of La Perche, the English Shire of Yorkshire, the Clydesdale of Scotland, to cite three of many. It should be remarked, however, that all of these horses, including the modern Ardennes or Belgian himself, are the product of major cross-breeding adventures with "warm-blood" horses. There are numerous great-horse types to be found elsewhere in Europe: the Jutland of Denmark; the Breton, Boulonnais, Poitevine, and Trait du Nord of France; the Niedersachen, Nöriker, Rheinland, and Schleswig of Germany; the Clydesdale of Ireland; the North Trotter and Ardennes of Sweden; the Suffolk Punch of Britain; and there are at least two distinct breeds of heavy draft horse considered indigenous to the Soviet Union.

The Pony

The differentiation of the giant of the species from the midget is, structurally speaking, merely a matter of degree. Paradoxically, there is a smaller difference between the great horse and the pony than between either and his "warm-blood" brothers.

The number of breeds of pony is perhaps even more astonishing than that of the great horse, if only because the uses to which the pony can be put have been more limited. About the only work a pony can do more effectively than, say, an Ardennes is to draw carts of ore out of a mine shaft, an assignment he

141

performed until the end of World War I in Britain, and even more recently in less developed countries.

Ponies are native to many isolated regions of Europe and Asia. If we accept the definition of a pony as any horse standing 14.2 hands or under, the range of types is truly extraordinary. Mostly "cold-bloods" in origin, like the great horses, European pony stocks are much more various and numerous in size, coat, conformation, and temperament than their larger relatives. The uses to which they have been put are also more diverse, and although the breeds remain fairly distinct from one another, there is little doubt that in some cases their bloodlines have been intermingled and that, in the case of the excellent little British hackney pony, to take the most brilliant example, important amounts of Arab blood have been introduced as well.

It is difficult to determine the antiquity of many pony breeds. Beyond the obvious fact that those of Europe's islands were imported at different early dates, the soundest surmise is that the Tarpan, closely resembling the original *equus caballus* (and sometimes confused with that primordial creature), sired the entire first pony breed. Feral Tarpans still run wild in parts of Poland and East Germany, where at least two other pony stocks also flourish—the Konik and the Huzul. In Germany, too, the Dülmen remains relatively more prolific than the vanishing strain of Senner ponies that inhabit that same region. In Austria, there is a separate breed known as the Hoflinger.

The very last vestige of the truly wild horse, *equus caballus prjewalskii*, of the Soviet Union, should also be classified by present standards as a pony.

In addition, that vast nation boasts two other distinct pony breeds, the Viatka and the Pechora. Scandinavia supports several varieties: the Fjord of Denmark; the Northlands, Westlands, and Döle-Gudbrandsal of Norway; the Gotland of Sweden. Dr. George Gaylord Simpson believes that the Icelandic pony may be the nearest surviving relative of the original Celtic pony. These animals were transported to Iceland, along with the original Norse settlers, in the eighth or ninth century and have maintained their integrity ever since.

In the Mediterranean estuary of France's river Rhône, the Camargue pony still grazes and breeds in comparative liberty. The Ariège pony of the Pyrenees lives in a somewhat more domesticated condition. The similarity between the Sarraia (or Garrano) of Spain and the Tarpan of central Europe has impressed many authorities; the connection between the two, however, remains largely conjectural, the most informed guess being that these ponies of Iberia were brought along from the steppes by the earliest protohistoric settlers of that region. The Minho of Portugal, in any case, does not very closely resemble his Tarpan-like Spanish neighbor.

The mountain pony of Italy is reminiscent of the ponies to be found on the mainland of Greece and the islands of the Aegean. Xenophon described three types of pony that were indigenous to his native land—the Achae, the Thessalian, and the Thracian. Doubtless the survivors in this area, the Pindos, the Panais, and the ponies mainly identified with the island of Skyros, are descendants of those three.

No region of the world abounds in a greater variety of pony breeds than the

142

British Isles. Five are to be found in England itself—the Dales, the Dartmoors, the Exmoors, the Fells, and the New Forests. Add to these the Welsh mountain pony and his rather more refined cousin, the Welsh pony; the Highland pony of Scotland; the Shetland pony of the islands north of John o' Groats; and the Connemara pony native to Ireland's County Galway—and there are ten.

The ponies found in Asia Minor and Major are, by comparison with their relatives in Europe, surprisingly homogeneous in appearance and size, the more so when we take into consideration the immensity of land mass and the diversity of climates of that great continent. Yet the explanation appears to be at hand: much of Asia has in common one kind of soil infertility or another, whether it be arid desert, alluvia, swamplands, or important extremes of altitude or temperature.

Although the pony stocks of Asia must surely have been crossed at times with "warm-blood" strains as the paths of Araby and those of Cathay were occasionally tangent, the lines of "cold-blood" or "warm-blood" in any presently flourishing breed are impossible to determine, mainly because records do not go very far back in the Near and Far East.

Turkey has only one authentic native pony breed, the Sivas, but it also has the half-breed Turkistan which is apparently a refinement of pony stock mixed with blood from an Arab, Barb, or Turkmene. India has two ponies, the Marwari and the Kathiawari, difficult to distinguish from each other. Similarly, despite their enormous expanses of territory and diversity of climates, China and Tibet possess only one native

143

144

pony each. Yet among the islands of Indonesia, isolation has produced no fewer than six types—the Sumba and Sumbawa, the Java, the Timor, the Batak, and the Bali. All are true ponies, clearly distinct breeds, even though only slightly different from one another.

The Arab, the Barb, and the Turk

Of the three horses that are the probable progenitors of the animal we admire today as the Thoroughbred, the Darley Arabian, according to tradition, came from the oldest and most elegant strain —the Persian Arab. This horse, just an inch or two taller than a pony, remains a distinct breed today. Thought to have been brought to the Near East something like fifteen hundred years or more before the epoch of Darius and Alexander, this excellent little horse is a superbly refined example of careful breeding. It is endowed with a small, aristocratic head, a glistening coat, a compact comformation, with prominent sinews of both fore and hind quarters— all characteristics of his "warm-blood" family style.

There is, in addition, an Egyptian Arab which is just a trifle smaller than his Persian relative—a more high-strung, more agile animal, with shorter hind quarters and a neck that arches more markedly. The Egyptian Arab is of more recent evolution than the Persian, very likely resembling the Kuhaylan of legendary Ishmael, and hence is probably similar to the *asil* of Mohammed's day.

As his name suggests, the Barb originated in Barbary, that portion of North Africa which borders the Mediterranean west of Egypt. He is one of the hardiest, strongest, and most versatile of horses. Pure Barbs are still produced

in both Algeria and Morocco. A variant, cross-bred from Arab and Barb, is preserved on a national stud farm in Libya.

Somewhat rangier, though not appreciably larger or more robust in appearance than the Arab and Barb, is the Turkmene, a horse still bred in the Soviet Union. His ancestry is not altogether ascertainable. One claim is that the Bactrian cavalrymen who served Darius rode Turkmene horses. Whether that is so or not, we do know that from this strain came the first and least consequential of the three sires that ultimately produced the first of the British Thoroughbreds.

The Thoroughbreds

All Thoroughbreds, by the definition in the first British General Stud Book (1791) and all other catalogs, are descended from three stallions imported into Great Britain during the late seventeenth and early eighteenth centuries. The conception of this breed is like the notion of morality; it results from a series of arbitrary definitions that conforms to "acceptable" practice and behavior at a given moment of social history. The evolution of the Thoroughbred is particularly interesting because it represents the first truly systematic development of a breed; all subsequent breeding practices owe much to this invention of the British.

The Thoroughbred is the oldest breed for which reasonably reliable records have been kept, and the line has probably been at least as carefully supervised as that of any royal or noble family. Like all well-established breeds, the Thoroughbred's is now a closed one; that is, both sire and dam of any foal must be registered in one of the acceptable stud books. In this respect, the blood lines of the Thoroughbred differ from those of man, where occasionally the names of the mothers are known but the fathers are unrecorded.

The first of the Thoroughbred's ancestors to appear in England was the Byerley Turk, named for a cavalry officer alleged to have acquired the horse as his portion of the loot from the successful siege of Vienna in 1686. During the final decade of the seventeenth century, Captain Byerley rode this handsome animal (whose provenience was doubtless the Turkmene breed) in the Williamite Wars against the Irish Catholic peasantry.

Although his seed was widely distributed, the Byerley Turk sired a line which does not bear his name but rather that of a son—Herod. Herod's progeny was preeminent in British and Irish flat racing throughout the eighteenth century. Track records show that Herod's heirs won something like 50 per cent of all the races for which there is fairly reliable documentation between 1775 and 1800. But this statistic may not be dependable, since it evidently includes races in which none of Herod's offspring were entered.

The Godolphin Barb (sometimes mistakenly described as an Arab) seems to be the ugly duckling of the original Thoroughbred line. According to the popular account, the stallion had been presented by the Emperor of Morocco to Louis XV of France. The king, a great horse fancier, seems to have been no better a judge of them than he was of women, for he is supposed to have thought the Barb an ungainly creature, unworthy for use as a sire in his royal stables; the Barb was disposed of in ignominious fashion.

When first observed in Paris by an English horseman named Cooke, a breeder by avocation, the wretched Barb was pulling a water wagon. Just what Cooke detected in this horse we cannot say. However, he purchased the animal and took him to his English country place in 1730. The shame to which the Barb was then subjected was perhaps greater than his honest French employment. He was used to test mares in season in order to determine whether or not they were ready for the services of Cooke's favorite stallion, Hobgoblin. As luck would have it, Hobgoblin refused one day to cover a mare called Roxana. The Barb was at last permitted to complete the act he had so frequently begun. The result of this coupling was a colt named Lath, which went on to become one of the most consistently successful flat racers of his generation. Thus did fame finally come to Cooke's Barb. In consequence, the owner sold him to Lord Godolphin, at whose stable the great stallion covered mares and himself with glory.

The Darley Arabian was acquired in 1704 at Aleppo by Thomas Darley, who was British consul in that storied Syrian city. The diplomat dispatched the young stallion to his father's estate in Yorkshire, where the animal sired a large number of colts and fillies that distinguished themselves on the racecourses of eighteenth-century England. His most celebrated descendant was Eclipse, generally regarded as the greatest and most colorful flat racer of the century. That horse's record on the track is staggering, even if we allow for the inflation that comes with legend. Eclipse is claimed never to have lost a race and never to have failed to start. Chroniclers tell us that in eighteen contests during the two seasons of his competitive

career, he never permitted a horse to pass him on the track and never required his rider to use either whip or spurs. Not only that, but we are asked to believe that Eclipse took his work so seriously that he attempted to kick and bite his rivals as well as outrun them. He remained at stud for eighteen years following his retirement from racing. From 1771 onward, Eclipse sired no fewer than 400 foals—an awesome get.

The three founding fathers of the Thoroughbred line produced generations of horses that were subsequently so cross-bred that by the end of the eighteenth century it was possible to say, as did the General Stud Book, that these stallions constituted the basis of the original Thoroughbred breed. As noted, however, the term "Thoroughbred" is a complete misnomer, since the mares covered by these great stallions and their progeny were of unknown and widely different qualities. Nonetheless, it is on this foundation that the Thoroughbred was officially predicated. Today, the breed is so widespread that its definition, except in racing circles, is blurred by its vastness. Besides, there are few saddle horses, hunters, steeplechasers, or pacers and trotters that do not owe many of their virtues to the fathers of the Thoroughbred strain. It is a heritage of the greatest significance to practically every other variety and style of horse in the world. There is ample substantiation for so extravagant a claim.

Thoroughbreds As Steeplechasers

The discovery that a Thoroughbred is a good hurdler or steeplechaser is frequently accidental. Animals that can run at great speed over a course that may be as long as four and a half miles, incorporating as many as thirty important obstacles (as in the English Grand National's test of endurance at Aintree), are always Thoroughbreds. Although ordinarily not quite swift enough to be effectively competitive on the flat, these horses are endowed with a natural

talent for jumping and with an impressive amount of stamina.

Almost every steeplechaser starts his career on the flat. Therefore, what is old for a sprinter may be young for a chaser. The latter normally begins to be tested over fences and hurdles at the age of five or six, by which age the average flat-racing stallion has been placed at stud or the mare at brood. The most successful chasers are, as a rule, geldings—a fact that is nothing less than tragic. One boggles, for instance, at the thought of the magnificent get that might have been sired by Arkle, the superb Irish steeplechaser of the mid-1960's, believed by many connoisseurs to be one of the greatest—if not the very greatest—ever raced. The defense for gelding a chaser stallion has two aspects. The first is that it makes his temperament less mercurial; and one must concede that a headstrong, unpredictable mount is probably not perfectly suited to leaping obstacles at speeds in excess of thirty miles per hour.

149

ABOVE: FINAL TURN AT THE BELMONT STAKES, ONE OF THE MAJOR EVENTS IN AMERICAN FLAT RACING. (UNITED PRESS INTERNATIONAL)

OPPOSITE: THE FINISH OF A RACE AT AQUEDUCT. (UNITED PRESS INTERNATIONAL)

The second defense is that a gelding tends more easily to put on weight and to retain it once gained, which enhances his staying power, especially for longer races. It seems a pity, all the same. For while there is an occasional mare that distinguishes herself over obstacles courses, as there are fillies that perform spectacularly on the flat now and again, the disciples of feminism in all living things will be disheartened to learn that the male horses are faster and stronger than the females.

Thoroughbreds As Flat-Racers

It is not possible here to offer a history of formal Thoroughbred racing. However, we may make some general observations about its terminology and practices in Europe and the United States. Flat races are run on grass or "dirt." In both cases, the surfaces are of special quality. There are relatively few grass tracks in the United States for economic as well as climatic reasons: the maintenance costs are high and the speeds attainable are not so impressive as those to be had on dirt. In the United Kingdom and Ireland, almost all courses are of grass. It survives better in a damp climate and can absorb average rainfall better than dirt.

The distances to be run are normally dependent on the age and/or experience of the horses in competition. It is usual for the younger animals to be raced at the shorter distances, called sprints. Distances for sprints are measured in furlongs—220 yards, a measurement that is one of the most ancient in use, going back to the days of the Romans. A furlong is at once one-eighth of a statute mile and one-tenth of the side of a ten-acre square. Sprints are ordinarily of 5 or 6 furlongs. Our ances-

tors in Europe and the United States were much more demanding of all their racing horses—notably before the closing of the Thoroughbred line. Races which consisted of heats of 4 miles each were not uncommon, allowing the contestant to rest for stipulated intervals between heats: 45 minutes between the four-mile races, for example. They were also less considerate about the age of the horses that they entered for these long distances; it is now generally thought scandalous to allow a horse of less than four years to run a long race, that being the age at which an animal is believed to have reached maturity. Young mares and stallions are fillies and colts in the vernacular of the track—remaining so until they begin their fifth official year of life. This is calculated in the United States and Europe from January 1st of the year in which the animal was born.

What has always made racing, and especially flat racing, a matter of such lively interest is, of course, the difference of opinion. Bettors have, at least from the time of the Romans, done all they legally and often illegally could do to shorten the real odds on the horses of their choice. Nothing is easier to fix than a horse race that is not adequately supervised—as we see in the chapter from *Mindy Lindy May Surprise* in the Appendix. Adequate supervision was impossible until the age of the electric starting gate, the photographed finish, and the motion picture (and now videotape) camera. Claims of illicit practice, like bumping, crowding, boxing-in, and holding a horse up were not easy to document. Even eyewitnesses, following each race with field-glasses, could be induced to perjure themselves if the price was right. Bookmakers, who

ABOVE: RACES AT EPSOM, BY GÉRICAULT, IS
A VIVID PAINTING EVEN THOUGH THE EARLY
19TH–CENTURY FRENCH MASTER DID NOT
UNDERSTAND THE MOVEMENT OF THE HORSE
AT THE GALLOP. (CLICHÉ DES MUSÉES
NATIONAUX)

OPPOSITE: GENTLEMEN'S RACE, BEFORE THE
START, BY EDGAR DEGAS, DEMONSTRATES
THE FRENCH PAINTER'S MASTERY OF THE
ATMOSPHERE OF RACING AND THE BEHAVIOR
OF HORSE AND RIDER. (CLICHÉ DES MUSÉES
NATIONAUX)

have flourished since Roman times, were not above making arrangements with jockeys and owners to assure minimal pay-offs.

Opportunities for larceny on various scales were exploited most zealously by racing enthusiasts in almost every country. When it proved impossible to corrupt a rider, an official of the track, or an owner, miscreants resorted to other practices that were frequently effective—the most popular being the drugging of a horse or "ringing," the substitution of animals so closely resembling each other as to be virtually indistinguishable. While these efforts were deplored by the gentlemen who, in the main, were owners of Thoroughbreds, they were difficult to suppress. Reports of misdeeds on the countless tracks that had sprung up all over the United States by the end of the nineteenth century were so numerous that in every state except Maryland and Kentucky flat racing was prohibited by law.

The principal complaint, from the outset, was a shameless manipulation of the odds by bookmakers. In 1908, science came to the rescue. For even in Kentucky, whose hospitable soil had long since proved one of the finest for the development of Thoroughbreds, there was so great an outcry against the activities of oddsmakers and bookmakers that the Kentucky Derby, the first and greatest flat race of any season, was apparently doomed in that year. The operator of Churchill Downs then put to use a primitive piece of machinery with which he had earlier experimented and put aside as too complicated. This was an importation from France, the *totalisateur*, or tote, a sort of computer which, under the name of *pari mutuel* (or mutual wager), could quickly shift the odds at the trackside as bettors placed their wagers on given horses. The Derby of 1908 took place as scheduled, and the success of the tote system was assured. Nevertheless, illicit offtrack betting continues to flourish illegally even in states where it has been legalized, mainly because a bookie may allow a bet on credit (which a state-owned establishment will not), and because large winnings obtained through a freebooting bookie are usually not reported as income for tax purposes. The Europeans, recognizing the impossibility of fairly collecting such taxes, have made gambling gains tax-free.

Truly dedicated followers of racing place at least some of their faith (in the form of cash) on the past performances of entries. For this purpose a number of publications came into existence—beginning with the General Stud Book of 1791, in Britain. "Dopesheets" that provide the gambler with the track records of all horses racing on a particular day (just as financial papers list the performance of all stocks traded) are compulsory reading for the regular bettor. The details tell him not only where each entry placed in his recent appearances but the distance of the race, the condition of the track, and the horse's immediate ancestry, as well as other factors that might affect the horse's chances. Much is made of track conditions. The "going" can indeed be crucial. Fastidious colts and fillies dislike the splashing of mud on their bellies and run with less enthusiasm when the track is wet, while others seem to enjoy it. Less experienced horses break less eagerly from the cells of the starting gate than older ones, and some gain reputations for breaking slowly later on. The talent of a renowned jockey will have considerable effect on the betting, especially since a highly successful rider will have a wider choice of mounts than the novice. The name of a horse's owner is also significant: some stables have become almost legendary producers of champions.

Breeders, for the most part, survive not so much by winnings from races in which their horses have prevailed as from the sale of stock descended from such animals. Blood lines are, of course, of great importance, but so too are the conditions under which foals are brought to maturity. The care given is tender and extremely attentive. Bloodstock sales, whether of mature or young horses—the latter mainly untested—bring prices that rise astronomically each year. So do stud fees, especially for the services of stallions that have had great and prominent triumphs. Foals descended from successful mares (notably Regret, the only filly ever to win the Kentucky Derby) do not command so ardent a market.

That flat racing is here to stay may be demonstrated by attendance figures at officially-sanctioned tracks all over the world, regardless of a nation's political orientation. The statistics for a recent year showed that upwards of 200 million people visited racetracks (other than those offering harness races), making racing by all measurements the most popular spectator sport on earth.

Steeplechasing vs. Flat Racing

Steeplechasing and hurdling, while much more colorful and certainly more exciting than races on the flat, has not proved nearly so favored a diversion in the United States as in Europe, particularly in the United Kingdom and Ireland, where virtually all equine contests from November through March are over obstacles, culminating with the English and Irish Grand Nationals.

The reasons for this want of enormous public acceptance are probably several—not least that it is at once easier and harder to "fix" an obstacle race than one run on the flat. That is to say, you can probably arrange for a particular horse to fall in a steeplechase, but it is virtually impossible to assure that the same horse will not fall, so hazardous are these events. The amount of pure luck involved, for instance, in the winning of the Grand National at Aintree, where as many as thirty horses are the usual number of entries, is colossal. This is the cause for major imponderables, factors that the bettor is reluctant to contend with. Half the field can fall at a single fence if there is an especially awkward accident. Unless a runner is far ahead or far behind, he may be caught up in the traffic and thus be unable to avoid a similar fate.

Another aspect that makes this sort of racing more difficult to forecast is that, as we have said, horses used in it are geldings and mares that have attained their maturity. Though horses can, with proper treatment and regular exercise live to be very old indeed, they age differently from one another. Arkle, the great Irish chaser, was just coming into his prime at the age of ten when a cracked leg terminated his career.

Finally, from the point of view of

tion which may have some solution in the establishment of a stallion sperm bank.

The difference between hurdling and steeplechasing, incidentally, is one of degree of difficulty, the former being, as it were, the training ground for the latter. Hurdle races are over obstacles which are lower and less demanding than those provided on steeplechase courses. Since both have their origins in point-to-point races that grew out of hunting and cavalry exercises, the steeplechase presents a greater likeness to life than the hurdle race.

The last topic to be discussed under this heading, handicapping, which began in the middle of the eighteenth century both in Europe and America, has evolved from a primitive process of guesswork to one of considerable complexity. (Early American handicaps involved giving the less favored horses head starts.) The same general rules apply for handicapping flat-racers and steeplechasers, the principle being that the more successful horses should carry more weight than those which have not proved themselves. While differences of weight normally range from 10 to 15 pounds, the great Arkle won several steeplechase events carrying 35 pounds more than his nearest rival, and gave the impression that he could have triumphed even had he been hauling a milk cart as well. Yet bettors place not a little confidence in this official appreciation of each animal's capacities.

The White Lipizzaner and the Black Anglo-Norman

The horses ridden by the masters of the Spanish Riding School of Vienna are an extremely distinctive breed.

owners and riders, it is surely the danger involved that makes obstacle racing less attractive than runs on the flat. Further, because stallions are almost always gelded before their use for this purpose, only mares can be bred for steeplechasing. The breeder cannot know, in effect, until he has already found a stallion wanting as a sprinter, whether he has a talent for taking fences and hurdles—by which time he is no longer a stallion and thus is useless as a sire. It is a bizarre situa-

156

One has only to contemplate their exceptional sleekness and finesse to understand how much these creatures owe to the stock that established the Thoroughbred lines in Britain. The very name of the institution should also indicate the influence of both the Barb and Arab, horses brought to the Iberian peninsula by the Moors. To reinforce this evidence, we possess a few facts, such as the sixteenth-century foundation of the school. For this was the epoch when western Europe was dominated by Philip II of Spain, whose mastery spread to Italy, the Low Countries, portions of France, and much of the New World then under the white man's dominion.

We know as well that there was a special quality of horse bred at Lipizza, in modern Yugoslavia, long before the creation of the Spanish Riding School. In what is now Czechoslovakia there was a breed known as the Kladruber, and at Fredriksborg, Denmark, the Royal Stud of that land produced a line of stallions which shared in the founding of the animal now recognized as the Lipizzaner. Added too were mixtures of "pure" Arab blood and even traces of the Tarpan from the Fogaras Stud in ancient Transylvania. The Lipizzaner, then, is a central European cross-breed which, over the years, has become a distinct and distinguished entity.

From its establishment in 1564, directors of the Spanish Riding School have brilliantly developed their exhibitions into a form of breathtaking artistry, yet consistently succeeded in relating their objectives to the natural movements of the finest cavalry horse and the ablest cavalry rider. You never see a School's horse cheapened, for instance, by being compelled to "count" or to "answer" questions with motions of the head. The institution, which has survived the demise of the empire that created it and the Austro-Hungarian regime which so long supported it, is a living museum/theater occupying a splendid baroque building which was erected in Vienna in 1735.

Although early masters of the School were indeed Spanish, the performances

LEFT: A LIPIZZANER AS IT BEGINS A LEVADE, A CONTROLLED REARING MOTION TYPICAL OF THE SPANISH RIDING SCHOOL'S PERFORMANCES. (CULVER PICTURES)
RIGHT: ANOTHER SPECTACULAR DEMONSTRATION OF THE DISCIPLINE AND GRACE OF THE SPANISH RIDING SCHOOL'S LIPIZZANERS. (CULVER PICTURES)

THE THEME OF THE POACHER, BY JAMES WARD, WAS
EXTREMELY POPULAR AMONG 19TH–CENTURY BRITISH
LANDOWNERS. (DETAIL, TATE GALLERY, LONDON)

as they are now presented owe practically nothing to these founding fathers. The exercises so meticulously and stylishly executed today are derived in the main from two volumes, one by a Frenchman, the other by an Englishman, both published in the seventeenth century. The earlier work was written by Antoine de Pluvinel, personal riding instructor to France's King Louis XIII, probably that country's most enthusiastic royal horseman. The work, called *Instruction of the King in the Art of Riding*, appeared in 1626. Though pedantic in manner, the matter was important as a guide to elegant horsemanship. Even more influential, perhaps, was *A New Method and Extraordinary Invention to Dress Horses*, by the Duke of Newcastle. The term "to dress" in the title should be duly noted, for from it sprang "dressage" which is the quin-

tessence of the Spanish Riding School's display. However, it is from the earlier French work that most of the terms are drawn; as a result, many equestrian expressions are in that tongue.

Probably more romantic than most such anachronisms, the Spanish Riding School achieved a sort of apotheosis in the very final days of World War II, when Austria was being overrun simultaneously by troops of the Soviet Union and the United States. In an emotionally supercharged rendition committed to film, the account of the saving of the famous Lipizzaners of Vienna for the delight of the West at the expense of the East is well known to most horse lovers. This last-minute salvation was due to the efforts of America's most controversial commander in Europe, General George S. Patton, Jr., master of armored warfare and former cavalry officer, who saw to it that the animals were rushed

in early youth) are immediately relegated to less glamorous tasks, though many of these rejected Lipizzaners go on to become excellent hunters, jumpers, and occasionally brilliant three-day-event entries.

So demanding is the training of the Lipizzaner gray that it may take as long as seven years to complete. When one considers that, as a rule, this training only begins after a horse has reached the age of five or even seven, the time involved in bringing such an animal to the required state of perfection is better appreciated. Happily, the Lipizzaner is a long-lived and durable breed; it is not uncommon for them to continue to perform their subtle and theatrical *haute école* exercises for the public until they reach the comparatively advanced age of twenty-five.

Though a rude upstart in comparison to the Spanish Riding School, the Cadre Noir of the French Cavalry School at Saumur, founded in 1764 by Louis XV, was obviously inspired by its Viennese predecessor. The exhibitions offered by the Cadre Noir are very nearly as impressive. What it most conspicuously lacks is a setting even remotely resembling the beautiful hall in which the Lipizzaners are displayed.

As the name Cadre Noir suggests, the horses ridden by the equestrians of Saumur are black: Anglo-Norman crossbreeds that owe approximately equal debts to ancestors of Arab stock and to the great horses of La Perche and the Ardennes. The emphasis of the Cadre Noir has long been more on actual cavalry exercises than on the delicate dance-like maneuvers of the Lipizzaner grays. The movements of the black Anglo-Normans, while quite as flawlessly disciplined as those of the Vienna School, are

behind United States lines before they could be taken by the oncoming Russians. Miraculously, the superb School itself was largely spared.

No lover of the equestrian arts has visited the Austrian capital and seen an exhibition of the magnificent riders and the lithe white Lipizzaners without coming away with an impression of having witnessed a sort of deification of the horse's talents. Required of these animals that wheel and dance and leap with such balletic grace are not merely nimble movement and perfection of body control, but uniformity of size and coloration. The nearly pure-white grays that we associate with the Spanish Riding School's performers are a selection from many foals born at the establishment's present stud at Piber, in Austria. Colts and fillies unfortunate enough to be born with coats of a shade that is other than black (as all grays appear at birth and

jumping ring. Mares compete as absolute equals with geldings wherever manners and conformation are at least as important as speed and/or endurance. There are relatively few hunter stallions, for the identical reason that they are rarely seen as steeplechasers and hurdlers: the stallion can be much too unruly and undependable.

Unlike the Thoroughbred line, that of the hunter is not a closed breed. Indeed, strictly speaking, it is not a breed at all. Without seeing a particular horse in action, even the most astute judge of hunter flesh would be extremely hard-pressed to determine whether or not it is suitable for that purpose. One is simply unable to tell, merely by looking at an animal, if he would make a satisfactory hunter. Great hunters also come in a much wider range of sizes and shapes than do Thoroughbreds, measuring anywhere from just above pony size to heights in excess of 17.2 hands.

Apart from a capacity to surmount almost any type of obstacle or ditch one is likely to encounter in a rustic locale, what the hunter must principally possess is uncommon poise and patience, and a willingness to do virtually anything that is asked of him, mainly at a smart but mannerly canter, and occasionally at a full gallop. The most cherished hunters are not necessarily the sleekest or most refined in appearance. The Irish hunter, to take perhaps the greatest horse that little island habitually produces, is quite often a cross between a Thoroughbred sire and an Irish Clydesdale dam. He is thus endowed with the great horse's advantages of height, strength, and endurance, and the Thoroughbred's zeal, passion, speed, and agility.

The jumper, finally, is more simply

less dainty and less "tricky," if admirers of the Spanish Riding School will pardon this slightly disparaging adjective. The black horses leap, rear, buck, and kick on command, and are meanwhile able to execute many of the more graceful and classical dressage maneuvers as well.

Like the Lipizzaners which are discarded because of their unsatisfactory coloration, those Anglo-Normans which have too many traces of white on the wrong portions of their bodies are segregated and put to other uses. They make fine show jumpers and excellent three-day-event mounts.

The Hunter and Jumper

The sexual discrimination that is a reality of flat racing and steeplechasing is conspicuously absent in the hunting field, the Olympic competitions, and the

160

and readily defined than hunters or steeplechasers. He is just a horse that can almost always leap over the highest, most complicated, and most distractingly constructed and decorated of barriers. The operative words of this definition are "almost always." Refusal in a hunter is embarrassing and, in a competition, costly; but in a jumper, it can be catastrophic. Not only must he be strong but eager as well. He may display these characteristics in different ways, especially in the style he selects for going over the obstacles he encounters. The hunter and the steeplechaser tend to take fences literally in their stride. Since there is usually no great occasion for haste in the former, this easy manner makes for an exceptionally comfortable ride. For the latter, a single break in stride may not only lose a race, but quite possibly throw the precariously-seated rider from his back, too.

The show jumper is asked to deal with various barriers of a sort never experienced in the field by either hunter or steeplechaser. He must not only leap high, quickly and cleanly, but must cope with "problem" jumps—pairs and triples, for example, placed in such a way that he absolutely cannot take them in normal stride; he has to collect himself and perhaps even change leads between leaps—all this at the signal of his rider. Jumpers, therefore, often "rush" the first obstacle, then gather themselves abruptly immediately in front of it, pausing or hesitating ever so slightly. They must then literally hurl themselves over it by an act of main force, relying on their powerful hind quarters, because that little pause in which they have indulged themselves has cost them momentum which usually carries the hunter or chaser up and over. As far as the rider is con-

cerned, this bucking fashion of clearing a jump poses serious problems and often acute discomfiture. One should allow the horse as free a rein as possible—following Caprilli's dictum—so that his natural movement is in no way impaired. On the other hand, it is of course essential for the rider to remain on the horse's back. This can be difficult, especially if the mount refuses the jump, and most especially if that refusal comes as something of a second thought. The speed with which a jumper completes a course can be the deciding element in a competition.

It is perhaps germane to note here my own experience of jumping on the backs of hunters, steeplechasers, and jumpers, which leads me infinitely to prefer the hunter. He is by far the least temperamental and most predictable of the types, and thus the most easily managed.

IN CROSSING THE STREAM, AN EARLY 19TH–CENTURY ENGLISH PRINTMAKER, HENRY ALKEN, HELPED TO SATISFY THE VAST MARKET FOR HUNTING SCENES. (BRITISH MUSEUM)

161

Indeed, the competent hunter very frequently will manage matters himself, with little guidance or assistance from his rider, in the way described in the Appendix by Siegfried Sassoon. Under ideal conditions, a steeplechaser is very difficult to bring to a halt. Once in motion, he likes to go on running, and he must be fought hard if the rider means to stop him before he has galloped himself out of energy. A chaser that takes part in a morning's hunt will almost certainly conclude that he has been entered in a point-to-point race. He will set the bit between his teeth, if offered the slightest opportunity, and storm ahead, quite oblivious of his rider. The jumper, by and large and curiously, is the least predictable of the three, save for that rare and peerless creature that never refuses and hardly ever makes a mistake. In a sense, he is the most difficult to ride

just because of the uncertainties and whims of his character and, further, because of the absurdity of some of the obstacles he is called upon to leap over.

The Hackney, the Trotter, and the Pacer

In spite of the images so firmly fixed in our minds by films pretending to depict life in the early American West, it was customary for carriage horses to draw a vehicle at a brisk trot. The reason is not merely one of comfort for the passengers, nor does it spring from a humane desire to spare the horse. The fact, rather, is that a cantering or galloping carriage horse will soon wear out the harness and other accessories that connect him to the conveyance he is pulling. The sudden lurching forward lunges of the three-beat gaits place a great strain on straps and shafts. In addition, if a team

of horses is performing the work, there is the supplementary embarrassment of rhythm—or lack of it. For the gallop is the gait of equine panic, the gait of little or no control.

As the name of the hackney implies, he was one of the original cab horses. Heredity and rigorous training in youth (which is understandably frowned on by societies for the prevention of cruelty to animals) induce some hackneys to alter the trot they were born with, to rearrange the order in which they move their legs forward and, in some instances, to lift them much higher than is normal or natural. This gait is called a pace or amble.

Since the demand for useful hackneys arose in almost all areas where roads were usually passable to light vehicles, a great variety of horses falls into this category. A strong animal with an easy,

natural, and rapid trot, no matter what his blood lines, can make a satisfactory hackney. Since the advent of the motor car, the waning need for horse-drawn carriages has led to the preservation and systematic breeding of only the showiest performers. The majority of them, even of hackney ponies, owe as much to the Thoroughbred as to less aristocratic forebears.

The trotter, however, has become increasingly popular as a sporting animal in the United States, in certain European countries (particularly France and the Soviet Union), and in New Zealand. In Great Britain and Ireland, trotting races are practically unheard of, considered *infra dig*, and on the same low level as dog-racing—the betting sport of the lower classes. There is, nevertheless, some slight interest in harness racing recently expressed in Wales—inspired,

some think, by a passion for any sort of activity that might annoy the English.

We shall deal presently with the evolution of the American Standardbred harness horse, but it is worth observing here that in France, for instance, the trotter owes much to the sturdy and showy Anglo-Norman stock which supplies Saumur's Cadre Noir and to Thoroughbreds brought back to the continent from Britain in the last century. Most bizarre is the fact that France appears to be the only country left where organized trotting and pacing races are still conducted under saddle, though the practice was common in Europe and the United States well into the last century.

The well-bred trotter is a remarkable animal, capable of speeds at his prescribed gait that are astonishingly close to those managed by the fleetest Thoroughbred flat racer. Prior to 1885, trotters and pacers alike suffered from an occupational hazard, the "break." If the animal broke from trot to gallop, not only did he lose speed, but he menaced the vehicle and driver with upset. In the year mentioned, an American named John Browning, who had a purely avocational interest in harness racing, invented the hopple; this was a very odd-looking contraption of loops and straps suspended midway on the radii of forelegs and tibias of the hind legs, and interconnected in such a way that a break became practically impossible for a trotter, and much more difficult for a pacer.

The difference between the normal trot and the pace is that in the former the motion of the legs is diagonally forward; in the latter, the legs of each side move forward simultaneously. There used to be a great deal of debate about which is actually the more rapid gait.

LEFT: HUNTING SCENES ON THE COVER OF A 16TH– OR 17TH–CENTURY PERSIAN BOOK OF POEMS. ABOVE: DETAIL FROM THE SAME BINDING. (WALTERS ART GALLERY, BALTIMORE)

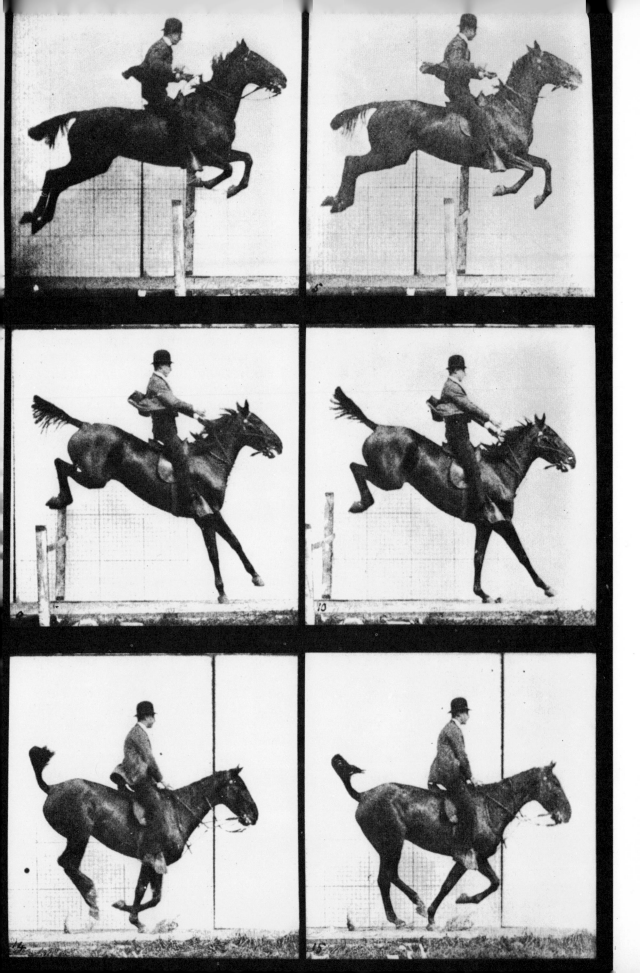

ANOTHER OF EADWEARD
MUYBRIDGE'S EXPERIMENTS
IN CAPTURING MOTION ON
FILM, THIS TIME OF A HORSE
TAKING A HURDLE.
(AMERICAN MUSEUM OF
NATURAL HISTORY)

There is no doubt that the pace is smoother—as the armored knights of the Middle Ages well appreciated. Since posting to a trot was out of the question when they were attired in their heavy gear, they greatly enjoyed the relatively bounceless motion of the pace. In essence, this gait is the foundation of the amble that is the chief distinction of the Tennessee Walking Horse, about which more will be said.

The point is well made, at all events, that a horse which has been trained to draw a carriage at a trot or a pace can almost always do so more rapidly and for greater distances and periods of time than he can at a canter or gallop, and more comfortably and more safely in the bargain.

The Polo Pony and the Quarter Horse

The polo pony is not a specific breed of horse. His position is precisely the same as that of the hunter. He is as good or bad as he is able to do. Further, if we accept the definition of the pony as a horse standing less than 14.2 hands, the polo pony is often not even a pony but a horse. He is a creature blessed with some exceptional mental and physiological qualities—powerful hind quarters which afford him very rapid acceleration, a pair of forelegs capable of extremely abrupt turns and rapid stops, a temperament responsive not only to the slightest touch of the bit but also to the nuances of leg pressure and the application of the reins along either side of his neck. This talent is described as being "bridle-wise" and only the dressage horse is required to possess it to a greater degree.

The size of the polo pony is a factor dictated more by the physique of the rider than by the sport itself. A player with a long reach is inhibited by a small mount; one whose arms are not long is under constant and needless strain if his horse is too tall. But the virtues of the pony are pretty well established. He must have stamina, fast acceleration, great agility and balance, and very steady nerves. The modern polo pony often shows the strong influence of the Arab or Barb, though the American Quarter horse is peculiarly suited to the sport and is more and more frequently used in the game, particularly in the Midwest and West of the United States.

The Quarter horse is a distinctly American development. Contrary to general belief, he was bred first in the East. The name "Quarter horse" first ap-

168

peared in print in 1833, with the publication of *The American Race-Turf Register, Sportsman's Herald, and General Stud Book*, a compendium produced by an Englishman, Sir Patrick Nisbett Edgar. Edgar's conscientious name for the creature was "the American Quarter Running Horse" by reason of its capacity to cover the distance of a quarter-mile at sensational speed. There is scarcely a Thoroughbred which could match the good Quarter horse over so short a course.

The Thoroughbred progenitor of the Quarter horse was Janus, a pony stallion imported to Virginia in the middle of the eighteenth century. Janus, described by his owner as a descendant of the Godolphin Barb, sired a great number of offspring in his adopted country, where he survived to the age of thirty-four. Many of these were characterized, in Edgar's words, by "great bone and muscles; round, very compact, large quarters, and . . . very swift . . . especially over short distances."

It may appear paradoxical that in a land so proudly, even arrogantly, prodigal of space as colonial America, the quarter-mile race should have been so popular an event. The explanation lay in the difficulty of clearing land and maintaining courses of greater length. On Long Island, not far from where the new Aqueduct Track is now situated, there was space for a four-mile oval, as there was in Maryland and Virginia, but these were distinct exceptions to the rule. The settlers of most sectors used the main streets of towns and villages as tracks for their contests. The Quarter horse was the drag racer of his epoch.

The genius for traveling short distances at extraordinary speed was not the sole virtue of the Quarter horse. As

AN AGILE QUARTER HORSE BRINGS HIMSELF UP SHORT. (BUDD STUDIOS, NEW YORK)

OPPOSITE: THE REARING OF THOROUGHBREDS REQUIRES MUCH PATIENCE AND CARE. HERE IN THE BLUE-GRASS REGION OF KENTUCKY, MARES AND FOALS GRAZE. WHEN THEY ARE OLDER, THE COLTS AND FILLIES WILL BE PUT TO THE TEST IN THE FIELD. (WALTER OSBORNE)

173

rodeo, but one that never fails to astonish because of the flawless harmony with which mount and rider function. It is easy to understand why the Quarter horse often makes so remarkable a polo pony. Moreover, a rider can sit his gentle trot all day.

Quarter horse races, so vividly described by Michael Erlanger in the passage to be found in the Appendix, continues to flourish in the West. Recent legislation provided for its reintroduction in the East. The quarter-mile race is the equine version of the hundred-yard or hundred-meter dash—enormously exciting, but ended almost before you realize it has begun.

The American Saddle Horse and the Tennessee Walking Horse

The breed now officially known as the American Saddle horse used to be called the Kentucky Saddle horse. Though his ancestry is obscure, his unique qualities are not, the most distinctive being the possession of five forward speeds instead of the usual three. Like the Walking horse from neighboring Tennessee, the American Saddle horse must be broken and specially trained in two eccentric gaits—the rack and the slow gait (the latter, also called the single foot, is a sort of broken amble)—despite the fact that generations of breeding have endowed him with a "natural" inclination to move in the unnatural manner required by the rack and slow gait.

Just why the rack was added to the repertory of the Saddler is uncertain. The most informed conjecture is also the simplest: It is an exceptionally showy method of propulsion, and it was developed to impress. It is, however, a gait that is uncommonly uncomfortable to sit for any lengthy period, and it is also

his descendants migrated westward with their pioneer owners, they were bred with horses of Spanish origins which had made their migration north from Mexico. The combination of the Spanish-Arab-Mexican cow-pony stock (first imported to the New World by Columbus and Cortes) with the progeny of Janus produced an animal that could outrun a stampeding herd of cattle or cut out the fleetest steer. Speed was enhanced by agility and courage. For once having isolated a single member of a herd, a Quarter horse must help his rider to control it, aid him with his roping, and maintain an ideal degree of tension on the *riata* while the calf is branded—an operation well known to followers of the extremely tiring for the horse. The slow gait, on the other hand, is an unusually pleasant one for the rider; we have no record of the horse's opinion of it. The action, as noted, is a close relation of the amble or pace that was bred into the horse many centuries ago. It is a means of locomotion which is useful for covering rough terrain without requiring the horseman to post.

An eighteenth-century Thoroughbred stallion named Denmark is held to be the single sire of the entire American Saddle horse breed. This contention, like so much other history, is belied by the very antiquity of Denmark's heritage and the fact that, descended from a nameless English dam and a Thoroughbred stallion, he was probably no better than any other animal which begat foals at about the same time. This decree of the American Saddle Horse Association was handed down in 1908, long after adequate evidence had disappeared. It was intended to resolve by fiat an argument that could not be settled by available data.

Essentially, the American Saddle horse —to the degree that he is a distinctive creature—is without great practical value. That is, he is mainly a show horse, bred and used exclusively for that purpose. Some Saddlers are converted to jumping; none are raced—though in show events the speed of the rack is one aspect of the Saddler's performance by which he is judged. Style, manner, and a remarkable verve are the features of the animal; he is the equivalent of the chorus girl in the show ring.

The Tennessee Walking horse seems to have emerged as a special breed toward the middle of the nineteenth century. His blood lines are much less rigorously decreed than are those of the American Saddler. He is acknowledged, in his present state, to have been sired by several varieties of stallion, notably the Morgan (of which, more later), the American Saddler, the Thoroughbred, and at least two kinds of pacers. The actual founding stock consisted of three stallions: Allan F-1, Back Allan, and Roan Allan. Today, there are more than 60,000 registered Walking horses, and the official register of the breed was opened only in 1935.

The walk of the Tennessee Walker is not the gait of the normal horse but rather, as suggested above, something like a stretched or overextended slow gait or broken amble. Bred originally as a plantation horse, one that could carry its rider over comparatively long, rolling distances at a reasonable but, above all, a comfortable rate of speed, the Walker in the field moves at something like 7

THE POSTURE OF THE RIDER OF THIS TENNESSEE WALKING HORSE INDICATES HOW EXTRAORDINARILY SMOOTH A GAIT THIS CREATURE MAINTAINS. (BUDD STUDIOS, NEW YORK)

or 8 miles per hour. When shown in the ring, however, the speed may be well in excess of 12 miles per hour, and therein lies a danger. The animal may, because he must stretch his legs extraordinarily to achieve such speed, kick his own hocks and thus lame himself. For this reason, during the period of training, the lower portions of each leg are protected.

The Walker is at his best when he is doing his specialty. There is probably no other horse so tractable for the novice rider or so easy to sit on for such long periods. Breeders of this admirable creature have an aphorism to the effect that if you ride a Walker today, you'll buy one tomorrow.

The American Standardbred

The American Standardbred is the principal trotting and pacing breed of the United States and the most influential harness racing stock in the world today. The founding sire was Messenger, imported to Philadelphia from Britain late in the eighteenth century. He is described by one contemporary as a "fleabitten" example of expendable British Thoroughbred, without any redeeming virtues. The Standardbred has a singular history in that Messenger is to this stock what the Byerley, Darley, and Godolphin stallions were to the Thoroughbred line. Like those animals, too, Messenger is enveloped in legend.

According to the records, which were kept in a most haphazard manner during the earliest period of American bloodstock breeding, Messenger sired more than a hundred foals in his career at stud in the New World. His personality is supposed to have been as unsavory as his get was great. At least one account depicts him as so unmanageable and vi-

cious that he frequently assaulted the stablehands assigned to care for him and that on one occasion he kicked a groom to death. Barney Nagler, turf analyst and chronicler of harness racing, dismisses this particular report as preposterous. Had Messenger really killed a man, he pronounces, the animal would have been put down forthwith. One cannot help wondering, all the same. A groom was easy to replace, but there could be only one Messenger.

The following decades produced a creature as elegant in appearance as the Thoroughbred, though with a conformation somewhat rangier, better adapted to the purpose of harness racing than the more compact descendants of the Turk, the Arab, and the Barb. Undoubtedly the most celebrated of nineteenth- and early twentieth-century lines of American Standardbred is the Hambletonian. These were fleet trotters which gave their name to the race that was long a feature of a harness track at Goshen, New York—an event shifted not too many years ago to the Midwest. The Hanover line of pacers has achieved greatness in recent generations.

The first of the trotters were used as fine carriage horses by the sporting enthusiasts of their day. The word "standard" in Standardbred was introduced to suggest that, when racing on straight or oval tracks was begun, a horse could pull a two-wheeled vehicle over a mile's distance at a stipulated rate of speed. The "standard" has been raised progressively over the years. Today it is 2 minutes 20 seconds, or a shade under 27 miles per hour.

Until the development in 1885 of the hopple, which was mentioned previously, it was unthinkable that a trotter (and more particularly, a pacer) could attain the present standard, so frequently did horses break from the designated gait. When a break occurs, the driver must pull his horse to the side of the track until it resumes the trot or pace. Many trotters and almost all pacers today wear the hopple. A second improvement was the advent of the bicycle-wheeled sulky, which replaced the high-wheeled affair that slowed the horse appreciably. This took place in 1895. Little more than a year after the introduction of the lighter, faster vehicle, the impossible had been accomplished—a horse had covered the mile in less than two minutes. This was managed in 1897 by Star Pointer.

The turn of the present century saw the appearance of Dan Patch, regarded by many experts as the greatest harness pacer of all time. In 1904, he set a record of 1 minute 56¼ seconds for the mile, a mark which stood for only a year, when Dan Patch lopped ¼ second from it. In 1906, when he was a nine-year-old, he ran the mile in 1 minute 55¼ seconds, a record which stood until 1938, when it was reduced by only ¼ second by Billy Direct. In modern times, pulling much more lightly constructed vehicles over improved tracks, only three other pacers besides Billy Direct have gone a mile more quickly than Dan Patch—Adios Harry, Adios Butler, and Bret Hanover, which established the current record of 1 minute 53⅗ seconds.

The argument about whether pacers are faster than trotters has been resolved in favor of the former, but mainly because the pacing action allows the animal to break from the start just fractionally more promptly than the trot. Greyhound, long regarded as the greatest of trotters, set a record for the mile in 1938 that stood until 1956, when

Noble Victory established a new mark of 1 minute 55⅗ seconds, a time bettered half a century earlier by the pacer Dan Patch.

The history of harness racing, especially in the United States, has been checkered, to say the least. Long beset by the same sorts of larcenous and mischievous conduct that afflicted Thoroughbred racing, it went into a sharp decline when the automobile began to assume the popularity as a racing instrument that the carriage had once enjoyed. Only at the beginning of World War II did harness racing cease to be merely a feature of county and state fairs and come into what we now recognize as its own. The turning point seems to center about the conversion of what is today called Roosevelt Raceway, on Long Island, from a road racing to a harness track. Since that time, in 1940, there has been no turning back. Today, in the United States, there are something like eight hundred harness tracks, most of them offering their cards at night (many think it was the introduction of lights that turned the trick). A second innovation, in 1946, was the automobile starting gate, which eliminated the countless false starts. A third has been the abandonment of heat racing except on what is called the Grand Circuit, where decisions are based on the best of three heats, a considerable reduction from the early number. In the main, each race is an entity—as with Thoroughbred events.

The Grand Circuit, established late in the last century, is organized along more or less the same lines as grand prix auto racing. The best drivers and horses move from track to track throughout the year, mostly to events associated with state fairs, about fifty in all, of which twenty are used in any year. Although

not major features of the enormous gambling "handle" attracted by harness racing, the Grand Circuit stakes have a unique prestige for horse and driver— none greater, perhaps, than that associated with the Hambletonian, now held in Illinois.

For reasons that are somewhat obscure, it is cheaper to own a stable of harness racers than one of Thoroughbreds, despite the fact that at least as much care and even more training is involved in their maintenance. Perhaps the explanation lies in the fact that harness racing is not so pretentious an enterprise as its more venerable competitor, that

it attracts working people who can attend only at night. Whatever the occasion, it is almost certainly more profitable to all concerned, for it attracts more than 20 million people annually in the United States alone. The sums legally wagered each year regularly exceed one billion dollars. It is a sport which also enjoys great favor in Europe, including the Soviet Union, where breeding of harness horses has made impressive progress and produced challengers that compete successfully in international contests staged in many countries. Only in France, as we have remarked, are trotting races still regularly offered with

178

riders instead of sulkies. No explanation has been given for this oddity.

Justin Morgan Had a Horse

The ancestry of Justin Morgan's superlative horse is unknown and surely will never be ascertained. Even the year and place of his birth are in doubt. All we know is that he was born some time between 1790 and 1795. How the young farmer-teacher-musician acquired the colt (some say it was a two-year-old when Morgan took possession) is questionable. In the absence of verifiable information, devoted students of the Morgan line concocted elaborate myths.

What is certain is that Morgan's stallion sired a trotting breed that is among the speediest, sturdiest, and most versatile of horses. The legend tells us that Morgan obtained the young horse as partial payment of a debt owed him by a man from East Springfield, Massachusetts. Because the colt had not yet been broken, the new owner is supposed to have led him all the way back to his home village of Randolph, Vermont. Once there, Morgan lost no time in harnessing him and setting him to the work of clearing stumps from the inhospitable northern New England soil, a task which the young stallion performed with astonishing eagerness and strength. Morgan called the horse Figure—a fact hardly anyone remembers any longer.

Figure was very small, almost a pony. He weighed less than a thousand pounds. Portraits of him are undoubtedly idealized, flattering to the point of being worthless. However, written descriptions ascribe to him a lean, clean head, like that of a Thoroughbred, though his body was said to have been more compact, resembling an Arab or a Quarter horse. The beguiling tradition is that Figure was blessed with sufficient stamina to work a full day pulling a plow or a farm cart and, afterwards, to draw or carry his delighted master over any required distance at a smooth but very brisk trot, his happiest gait. The tale adds that Figure could pull a light buggy over a measured mile in 3 minutes, a claim properly rejected by skeptical scholars, who think that the time of 4 minutes is much more probable, especially considering the likely weight of the vehicle and the terrible conditions of the roads in outland Vermont at the turn of the nineteenth century. We must also bear in mind that Dan Patch, surely endowed with Morgan blood, managed to cover a mile in a little less than two minutes under the best of conditions.

When Justin Morgan fell upon evil times and began to suffer ill health, he leased Figure out to a farmer of the neighborhood, Robert Evans, for whom the stallion did the work of an ordinary farm horse. But Evans was not long in appreciating Figure's truly remarkable virtues. One anecdote recounts a wager of a gallon of rum that the horse, after a full day's work, could not pull a huge pine log to a sawmill from the point where it had been felled—a log which other individual horses, fresh from a night's rest, had been unable to budge. Evans not only accepted the challenge but suggested that three of the doubters sit on the log while Figure made his attempt. Of course, the little stallion easily drew the log and its drunken passengers the full distance to the mill. It is of such stuff that the legends of Paul Bunyan and his great blue ox were concocted in the same era.

Justin Morgan died in 1798, in the residence of the local sheriff to whom he had given Figure as payment for care and lodging during his last illness. Hardly was Morgan in his grave before the peace officer put the stallion up for auction. His purchaser was Robert Evans, who plainly knew better than anyone else the true worth of this nearly miraculous creature. The selling price is not established, nor can we say at what point Figure came to be called "Justin Morgan's horse" and, ultimately, "Justin Morgan." Thus did an obscure country schoolteacher attain a sort of immortality. The animal did for him what Alexander the Great had done for Bucephalus.

Robert Evans worked his new stallion in his fields, and then entered him in the pulling contests and the informal trotting races that were among the warm-season features of Vermont life. Justin Morgan's reputation for speed, strength, and tractability spread throughout the state and the rest of northern New England. Consequently, he was invited to cover a wide variety of mares. We are to believe that almost every foal he got resembled him much more than its mother, so dominant were this stallion's genes.

Descendants of the celebrated Justin Morgan, notably Sherman Morgan, sired a line of sensationally successful trotters that owed not a thing to Messenger, so far as anyone is aware. Justin Morgan outlived his master and namesake by twenty-three years. His final days were spent at Randolph and nearby Chelsea where, true to the flavor of the legend which he had become in his own time, he is supposed to have perished from neglect. No skeptic, however, can take from this stallion a patch of his greatness. He was surely the most astonishing horse of his time. His off-

spring continue to be as versatile and as amenable to all sorts of travail as he was himself. For example, most police horses in the United States are of Morgan blood—stable and good-tempered under very difficult conditions. All the same, very few Morgans are asked to do farm work any longer.

The Appaloosa

The first description of the Appaloosa horse appeared in the journal of Meriwether Lewis, who saw this curiously colored breed in the late winter of 1806, when he and William Clark were nearing the end of their tortuous journey to explore the Northwest Territory for President Jefferson. In an upland valley, near the confluence of the Palouse and Snake rivers, the travelers came upon a large settlement of Nez Percé Indians, a nation of hunters and salmon fishermen. Their horses, Lewis wrote, appeared "to be of excellent race; they are lofty, eligantly [sic] formed, active and durable; in short, many of them look like fine English coarsers [sic] and would make a figure in any country. Some of these horses are pied with large spots of white irregularly scattered and intermixed with a black, brown, bey or some other dark color. . ."

What distinguishes the Appaloosa from all other Indian-bred horses is more than his conformation and color, though one must be a little perplexed by Lewis' description of the creature as "lofty," for he normally stands only 15 hands, just 2 inches taller than a pony—hardly a "fine English coarser." The great difference is that the Appaloosa was and remains a horse that has been bred in a systematic way, a practice not followed by other tribes. The Nez Percés had discovered, about three-quarters of a

WITH THE COMING OF THE AUTOMOBILE, THE HACKNEY PONY BECAME A SHOW ANIMAL, WITH GAITS MUCH FLASHIER THAN THOSE OF HIS ANCESTORS, DRAWING VEHICLES MORE NOTABLE FOR APPEARANCE THAN PRACTICALITY. (WALTER OSBORNE)

century before the appearance of Lewis and Clark, the secret of selectivity. The result of this revelation, the horse which takes its name from the Palouse River where it was developed, is distinctive for the shape of the head as well as steadiness of temperament, sturdiness, and remarkably varied coloration.

That this admirable breed should have survived the vicissitudes to which the Nez Perces were subjected by generations of capricious and greedy white settlers is a tribute to the fortitude and spirit of the tribe. In the nineteenth century, Chief Joseph, the last great sachem of that Indian nation, described the nature of the bargain his people had made with the authorities who represented the intruders. We quote him here because he used the analogy of horse trading, about which he knew a good deal:

If we ever owned the land we own it still, for we never sold it. In the treaty councils the commissioners have claimed that our country has been sold to the Government. Suppose a white man should come to me and say, "Joseph, I like your horses and I want to buy them." I say to him, "No, my horses suit me. I will not sell them." Then he goes to my neighbor, and says to him: "Joseph has some good horses, but he refuses to sell." My neighbor answers, "Pay me the money, and I will sell you Joseph's horses." The white man returns to me and says, "Joseph, I have bought your horses, and you must let me have them." If we sold our lands to the Government, that is the way they were bought.

The parallel drawn by Chief Joseph was a fair one. In 1877, the Nez Percés who declined to accept the white man's religion and rule, and refused to re-nounce their practices of breeding horses and cattle, were ordered to the Lapwai Reservation in what is now the state of Washington. Violence ensued and continued intermittently for about eight years. In 1885, Chief Joseph, his warrior ranks depleted, allowed what remained of his tribe to be consigned to the Lapwai and Colville reservations. In view of the horrendous half-century of harassment the Nez Percés had endured, it is nearly miraculous that they should have succeeded in maintaining the Appaloosa breed, the more so since, in his surrender to the whites, Chief Joseph had been forced to give up to the conquerors more than a thousand head of his precious horses and a hundred saddles.

The Appaloosa's popularity was for a long time primarily a regional phenomenon, confined to the northwest, until Buffalo Bill Cody focused attention on the breed by riding only Appaloosas in his famous Wild West shows. By the early years of the present century, the Appaloosa had a global reputation, fostered by his distinctive appearance, but based mainly on his stamina and agility. It was not, however, until 1938 that the Appaloosa Horse Club was established, and only in 1950 that the breed was accepted by the National Stallion Board as a genuine purebred strain.

The Pinto and the Palomino

"Glory be to God for dappled things," wrote the poet Gerard Manley Hopkins. Though this notable English mystic was expressing gratitude for more than merely the piebald horse, the reference is germane, because he was thinking of creatures generally rejected by society as imperfect or impure—the various

IN THE WHITE HORSE, *PAULUS POTTER, A 17TH–CENTURY DUTCH ARTIST, PAINTS AN ENGAGINGLY SPOTTED ANIMAL. (CLICHÉ DES MUSÉES NATIONAUX)*

sorts of "freckled" things that nature produces. Piebald horses, especially if they turned up as the foals of Thoroughbreds, trotters, American Saddlers, or even Quarter horses, customarily were greatly deplored. The peerless ancestor of all the fast breeds, the Arab, is distinguished, among other things, for his black skin. This has no bearing on the color of his coat, which is invariably solid. The only acceptable mottling of the Arab is that of the gray; all others must be of a uniform hue, save, perhaps, for traces of white on face and feet.

The evolution of the piebald horse, the Appaloosa and the Pinto, as a mount suitable for a "gentleman," is a tale that had its beginnings in early American colonial days, when any horse was better than no horse at all. In Africa and Europe, there certainly had long been piebald horses, but their breeding had been actively discouraged. In the Americas, where the horse was doubly treasured because of the enormous tracts of land a proprietor needed to protect in order to assure his possession of it, there was no such effete constraint on their proliferation.

It appears that the Pinto (the word is a contraction of the Spanish *pintado*, meaning "painted") was partly the result of the horse's devolution in grazing lands which were under the control of the Indians. The Pinto is not a breed, but a type. The Appaloosa, for instance, is also a Pinto. Except for the multicolored horses that enjoyed favor in the circus rings of Europe, there was no vogue for this sort of animal until well into our own era. He is commonly of the size of the Quarter horse and the Appaloosa, and may be put to a variety of uses, especially as a cow pony or saddle horse.

The Palomino, on the other hand, is very much a breed. He is remarkable not only for the pale buffs, buckskins, and near-mauves of his coat—and, without variation, for his blond mane and tail—but also for his striking resemblance to the Arabs and Barbs of which he is an offspring, with not a few additions from some of the great-horse strains of northern Europe. Selective breeding has produced a handsome and exceptionally showy creature, often a first-rate jumper, but above all a fine saddle and parade horse.

It is essential to repeat, following this brief survey of the breeds and types of horse and pony, that volumes have been devoted to individual breeds and even to the careers of single horses. I have tried simply to indicate the range and variety. The numerous forms of the horse today are wholly a creation of man, of his care and attention. So there is something ironic in the fact that this wonderful animal, so scrupulously cultivated for so many centuries by affectionate and dutiful husbanders, is still born as free in spirit as the foals of the Siberian wild horse. True, the hunter colt has in his genes a latent talent for the hunt, the Thoroughbred for racing, the Quarter horse for the tasks of the corral and for polo. But each new generation of horses, regardless of its refinement and lengthy bloodlines, must be domesticated. And each new generation, no matter how remote from its ancestors now grazing in northern Asia, would begin to revert to type if permitted to flourish according to the natural dictates of herd life.

In the choice of a horse, the principal consideration must be the use to which the purchaser means to put him, a decision which will necessarily be influenced by whether or not one is a highly or only a moderately skilled rider, if riding is the purpose intended. The prospective horse-buyer will not find in these pages anything of solid use except a single piece of advice: If you know little about horses, by all means secure the assistance of someone who knows much, someone, moreover, whom you can trust.

Among purveyors of commodities, horse traders enjoy a unique reputation for telling eager purchasers less than the entire truth about the creature being offered for sale. If a horse trader was not the author of the phrase *caveat emptor*, then one of his duped customers surely must have been. However, there is a very curious difference in the attitude assumed by the client who has been gulled by a seller of any other object from that of the person who has been had by a horse dealer. The former is rightly and sometimes righteously indignant over having been cheated; the latter is frequently rather philosophical. Indeed, it seems that for centuries the disappointed horse-buyer has almost taken a sort of masochistic satisfaction from the duplicity of the man who sold him a beast that proved not to be as advertised. While there have assuredly been some major exceptions (horse dealers have been murdered by disgruntled victims), one might dare to suggest that a quality of minor martyrdom attaches to the purchaser who has been taken in by a dealer's misrepresentation of a horse. A little literature of folklore has grown up about the shrewd horse trader, its ancestry as ancient as the written word.

THE HORSE
IN ART

HORSES AND POETS SHOULD BE FED, NOT OVERFED.
CHARLES IX OF ENGLAND

This chapter discusses a very modest sampling of the immense quantity of art in which the horse has figured. The emphasis is not simply on the horse, but also on the manner various artists have chosen to make use of the horse as symbol or ornament.

When did art begin? The question has never been satisfactorily answered by archeologists, anthropologists, or historians of art. At what point did pictorial art—for instance, the illustrations and inscriptions on the walls of ancient caves —cease to have a purely historical or religious significance and become "art," work accomplished merely to please the eye of the beholder? Since we are concerned here exclusively with representations of the horse, regardless of their intended use, we fortunately need not attempt to answer the question.

In earlier chapters there are many illustrations of horses that are indeed art. In the second chapter, for example, some of the pictures derive from the great artistic wealth of early civilizations. A few initial efforts are crude, unschooled attempts to tell stories in which the horse played a role of some importance. Whether carved or painted on walls, or sculptured like the extraordinary little Cypriote statuette of the tenth century B.C. (page 17), the artist had problems in mastering the anatomy of the horse. Many depictions from ancient Greek amphorae and craters (pages 19, 30–31), however, are far more refined than much that was produced during the Christian Middle Ages in Europe.

For reasons that can never be completely explained, the Greeks, especially those of the region around Athens called Attica, managed to create in the brief era which Alexander the Great dominated an exceptionally rich culture. Almost all the arts and crafts we treasure today found their very first expression in ancient Greece. From the next period, called Hellenistic, when Romans had

PRECEDING PAGE: RIDER, 1941, BY MARINO
MARINI. (PHOTO: CONZETT & HUBER, ZURICH)
ABOVE: EIGHT HORSES (DETAIL), BY CHAO
MENG-FU. (METROPOLITAN MUSEUM OF ART,
KENNEDY FUND)

186

ABOVE: HORSES CROSSING A RIVER *(DETAIL)*,
*BY CHAO MENG-FU. (FREER GALLERY OF ART,
WASHINGTON, D. C.)*
LEFT: WASHING HORSES IN A RIVER *(DETAIL)*,
*BY CHAO MENG-FU. (METROPOLITAN MUSEUM
OF ART, H. O. HAVEMEYER COLLECTION)*

187

OPPOSITE: *DETAIL FROM A MINIATURE IN* THE TALE OF AKBAR, *A 16TH-CENTURY PERSIAN WORK. (VICTORIA AND ALBERT MUSEUM)*
BELOW: THREE SONS OF SHAH JAHAN. *PERSIAN MINIATURE.* *(VICTORIA AND ALBERT MUSEUM)*

conquered Greece, comes the frieze from the Greek temple of Artemis (pages 34–35). Nothing the Romans themselves fashioned was finer than this.

While Europe entered the so-called Dark Ages, the period of the Barbarian conquests, the countries of the Near and Far East produced paintings, ceramics, and sculpture of great sensitivity and artistry—as in the work of the Chinese T'ang Dynasty (618–906). The mass and vitality of the three terracotta horses shown on pages 42 and 43 are typical of the attainments of Oriental civilization in that period.

Westerners nevertheless persist in conceiving of art as having been much more a European than an Oriental accomplishment. Evidence abounds that this is far from the truth. Islamic art, such as the scene from the *Tale of Akbar* and the *Three Sons of Shah Jahan* prove that in the Fertile Crescent much wonderful work was being done while Christian monks were struggling over their illuminated manuscripts—masterpieces in their fashion, to be sure, but seriously wanting in exuberance and scope and in knowledge of such technical fundamentals as the conformation and articulation of the horse. The paintings of Chao Meng-fu, a Chinese master of the thirteenth and early fourteenth centuries, are equally convincing evidence that "art" was far from a European patent.

Yet it was from medieval craftsmen and from classical Greek and Roman relics unearthed in Italy, together with some influential information gathered by the Crusaders in the Near East, that the artists who would lead European culture out of the Middle Ages into the Renaissance derived their skills and a good deal of their subject matter. In the illustrations from a variety of

centuries, the majority of artists showed all historical and religious occurrences as having taken place in the trappings of ancient Rome.

So, indeed, did the artists who created the Renaissance in Italy, France, the Low Countries, and Germany. The great historian Jacob Burckhardt dates the onset of this culturally revolutionary period to the late thirteenth century in Italy. Art historians, somewhat more conservative, consider artists of the late fourteenth and early fifteenth centuries the true innovators.

Although some celebrated names are associated with the very beginnings of the Italian Renaissance in art, those whose paintings and sculptures illustrate this chapter flourished from the fourteenth century onward. The first was the Veronese painter Stefano de

illuminated manuscripts, most notably from *The Book of Hours of Catherine of Cleves* (pages 39, 49, and 50), we note themes that were to be reiterated throughout the Renaissance and after: Saint George and the Dragon, Saint Martin and the Beggar, and the Conversion of Saint Hubert—holy men closely associated with the horse and usually depicted in the company of a horse.

Medieval scenes were not always devoted to sacred subjects. War was a frequent source of inspiration to early illuminators. And it was only in the late eighteenth century that artists began to provide images of historical and religious incidents in a manner reasonably faithful to the actual circumstances. Until then, one had to be content with views that were contemporary in matters of costume and architecture. For the better part of the seventeenth and eighteenth

190

Zevio, whose *Horses and Riders* is a fine example of the transition from medieval to Renaissance styles.

From the first half of the fifteenth century come works by Uccello and Pisanello, the latter much more the master of classical form than the former. Pisanello's *Vision of Saint Eustace* (page 52) shows us a horse that is well observed, though hardly a lifelike rendering. Uccello, on the other hand, was much more audacious and his view of life was more vital and exciting. His *Night Hunt* (pages 162–63) is one of the first attempts to portray a scene taking place in darkness. Uccello's horses seem rather like caricatures of the creature we are familiar with, but he did try to show the animal in attitudes captured only rarely and timidly by other western painters of his era.

Italian artists whose careers spanned the second half of the fifteenth century made significant strides in their treatment of the subject and their ability to depict anatomically accurate images of the horse. By this time, Italian artists had attained so high a degree of craftsmanship that it was no longer a serious problem for the most proficient of them. Many questions concerning the arrangement of space, perspective, and proportion had already been answered. This period is the beginning of what has been termed the High Renaissance.

One of the first great painters of this epoch was Andrea Mantegna, whose imaginative illustration of the legendary Mount of Parnassus appears on page 48. The painting is vividly visionary, and we are charmed by the artist's impression of the winged Pegasus, shown as an equine bird, complete with feathers and a curiously benign expression for a steed reputed to be so fiery.

191

SKETCHES OF HORSES, BY LEONARDO DA VINCI. (ROYAL LIBRARY, WINDSOR. BY PERMISSION OF H. M. QUEEN ELIZABETH II)

193

TOP: *HORSE AND RIDER FALLING,
A SKETCH BY TITIAN. (ASHMOLEAN
MUSEUM, OXFORD UNIVERSITY)
BOTTOM: STUDY OF A HORSE, BY
MICHELANGELO. (ASHMOLEAN
MUSEUM, OXFORD UNIVERSITY)*

Master to several younger artists was the Florentine Verrocchio, the greatest sculptor of his fifteenth-century period, and probably best remembered for a great equestrian statue in Venice. The sketch of a horse shown in this chapter is interesting chiefly for the artist's anatomical notations. Verrocchio's attempt to understand the physiology of the horse was more successful than that of any other artist of the entire Renaissance period—with a single exception.

The exception was Verrocchio's most notable pupil and perhaps the greatest man of the entire Renaissance, Leonardo da Vinci, the sublime Florentine. So much has been written of him that all we need add here is that his studies of the horse, of which some are to be seen in this chapter, are remarkable not only for their fidelity to the horse's conformation, whether at rest or in motion, but also for the daring of his conceptions. Not until the availability of stop-motion photographs of the horse's movements could we appreciate the accuracy of his observations.

It has been said of Leonardo that he devoted so much of his time to study that he left us comparatively few finished works. The assertion is just. No other major master has bequeathed so small a legacy of completed paintings and sculptures. A study for an equestrian statue of the Sforza master of Milan is an example of the sort of problem that Leonardo set for himself. The work was to be of truly epic proportions, but it was never cast. We do, however, have a small bronze figurine of a rearing horse that was finished by Leonardo, startling for its clinical accuracy and for its excitement. After his death in France in 1519, artists all over the Continent spent lifetimes attempting to recapture

one aspect or another of Leonardo's extraordinary powers of analysis and rendering.

Art was not standing still in the rest of continental Europe while the masters of the High Renaissance in Italy were accomplishing miracles of innovation to dazzle their patrons and visitors from foreign lands. Among those who came to Italy was the German Albrecht Dürer, one of the first and finest of early print-makers. There is a richness of fantasy which informs much of his work, a quality to be seen in *The Knight, Death, and the Devil* (page 68) and *The Four Horsemen of the Apocalypse* (page 69).

SEVEN HORSES FIGHTING IN A WOOD, *BY HANS BALDUNG.* (*METROPOLITAN MUSEUM OF ART, H. B. DICK FUND*)

195

Although the sixteenth century would see Renaissance modes of art spread throughout Europe, it was an age in which most of the giants were Italian. Raphael, had he lived to old age, might well have become the greatest artist of his time. He died, however, in his thirties, leaving a body of work that is staggering in its volume and variety. His famous painting, *Saint George and the Dragon* (page 51), is one of his noblest tributes to the horse and an admirable example of the cool, rational, smooth style of classicism that was to make Raphael an idol to artists for two centuries after his untimely death.

The names we usually associate with the evolution of the High Renaissance styles into its Mannerist and Baroque variations are Titian and Michelangelo. The Florentine Michelangelo's work was rather a summary of all that had happened to art during the two centuries before his birth in 1475. It is technically incorrect to allude to him as a romantic figure, for the romantic movement lay well in the future; yet his was a romantic nature, mercurial and quixotic, and these qualities show themselves in his work. The drawing of a horse attributed to him is a creature in harmony with the convoluted beings that populate his few paintings, his vast frescoes, and his protean sculptures.

Michelangelo was first and last a sculptor. His slightly younger contemporary, Titian, was solely a painter. Michelangelo's greatest concern was for the supremacy and integrity of line. Titian thought color the single most critical element of painting; his drawing, *Horse and Rider Falling*, is something of a rarity. Though the two men are thought to have met only once, if at all, the argument produced by their diver-

gent opinions has never been satisfactorily resolved, nor has it really needed to be. One could be a colorist without abandoning respect for form and space; the other could be a master draftsman without sacrificing the emotional impact effected by color.

Likeness to life was a passion of the Alsatian Hans Baldung, trained in Germany but heavily influenced by Italian thematic material. Like so many northern European artists of his day, he was a realist, as can be seen in his work, *Seven Horses Fighting in a Wood.*

To the other artists of the sixteenth century whom we will discuss, realism was less and less important a factor. El Greco's career is in many ways the strangest of any Renaissance artist. He was born in Crete, he studied with Titian and Tintoretto in Venice, and he passed the last half of his life in Toledo, former Spanish capital and still seat of the all-powerful Church—a city of enormous intellectual cultivation where, however, no major artist had ever before settled. Working by himself, under virtually hermetic conditions, El Greco produced work that was more and more

LEFT: EQUESTRIAN PORTRAIT OF CHANCELLOR SEQUIER, BY LEBRUN. (CLICHÉ DES MUSÉES NATIONAUX) MIDDLE: CHARLES I OF ENGLAND, BY ANTHONY VAN DYCK. (NATIONAL GALLERY, LONDON) RIGHT: GEORGE III OF ENGLAND AT THE BATTLE OF DITTINGEN (DETAIL), BY JOHN WOOTTON. (NATIONAL ARMY MUSEUM)

LEFT: EQUESTRIAN STATUE OF LOUIS XIV, BY FRANÇOIS GIRARDON. (CLICHÉ DES MUSÉES NATIONAUX)

197

ascetic and mystical. Because of his isolation and his failure to secure the favor of the greatest of all royal collectors of the age, the Spanish King, Philip II, his achievement had no influence on the development of art in his adopted country. After his death in 1614, he was forgotten. His rendition of the legend of Saint Martin and the Beggar (page 61) was painted in the middle of his long stay at Toledo. The figures of men and horse show not only his lack of interest in likeness to life (a quality which later endeared El Greco to the Post Impressionists), but also his obsession with the emotional power of color at the expense of line.

With the beginning of the seventeenth century, the art of Italy went into an eclipse that lasted until our own era. It can be explained more in terms of politics and war than of art itself. Italy became a museum and an academy of art, attracting young craftsmen from all over the Continent to see the wonders that had been produced there in earlier periods; but the country was incapable of developing new masters of its own.

Many artists composed great works during the seventeenth century in other European countries. However, since our subject remains the horse, we must confine our view to a handful of masters. The first is the Flemish Rubens, best recalled for his fleshy nudes. As a painter of horses (page 107), he was chiefly important for a style that would influence painters of the nineteenth century, especially in France.

The career of Anthony van Dyck was marred by lost promises. He was the finest of Rubens' pupils and would have succeeded to his master's hugely profitable practice had he not been rashly indiscreet (or so Rubens imagined) in

DRAWINGS OF NOBLES PRACTICING HORSEMANSHIP, AS SEEN BY THE JAPANESE MASTER HOKUSAI (1760–1849).

LEFT: HORSE FRIGHTENED BY A LION, *BY GEORGE STUBBS. (WALKER ART GALLERY, LIVERPOOL)*
RIGHT: THE NIGHTMARE, *BY HENRY FUSELI. (GOETHE MUSEUM, FRANKFURT AM MAIN)*
BELOW: A HORSE, *BY THÉODORE GÉRICAULT. (NATIONAL GALLERY OF IRELAND, DUBLIN)*

his relations with the great painter's first wife. Later, van Dyck established himself in London where, like Rubens, he was knighted by Charles I, whose renowned equestrian portrait is reproduced in this chapter. Though he was far from attaining the understanding of equine anatomy that Leonardo had possessed a century and a half before him, it was van Dyck in particular who introduced horse painting to England. He fully expected to return to Antwerp on Rubens' death, but followed his former master to the grave only a year later.

The painter who probably least typifies the ebullience and optimism of the expansive seventeenth century in western Europe was Rembrandt. He never visited Italy, hardly traveled at all outside of his native Netherlands, and looked ever more inward as he aged and saddened. Even when he was compelled to do subjects like the horse, as in his popular picture called The Polish Rider

(page 56), the degree of introspection is astonishing. The ungainly little mount seems as pensive as its master.

Perhaps the most surprising artistic development of the eighteenth century was not the appearance of Francisco Goya's single brilliant star in a dark Spanish firmament, but the discovery of an entire but short-lived constellation in Great Britain. The period saw the rise of a number of skilled painters of the sporting scenes so dear to the hearts of the English country gentleman. George Stubbs, who is also represented on page 144, was doubtless the most popular horse painter of the century in his native land. A keen observer of equine behavior, he evoked, in *Horse Fightened by a Lion*, emotions frequently evinced but seldom captured on canvas.

One of the master sculptors of the eighteenth century in France was Edmé Bouchardon, whose heroic equestrian statue of Louis XV appears on page 196.

Two bizarre figures marked the turn of the nineteenth century in England, though they were really products of the previous era: William Blake and Johann Heinrich Füssli (whom the English soon Italianized as Henry Fuseli). Blake was surely the more exceptional of the pair. An engraver by trade and a metaphysical poet by nature, he was an artist of unique religious vision. He is represented in this book by *God Creating Adam* (page 219). Blake was treated by some of his contemporaries almost with contempt, and it was not until the beginning of our own day that the quality of either his poetry or his art was fully savored.

Fuseli, descended from numerous German-Swiss artists, came to England in the 1780's and soon established himself as an artist of considerable popular-

ity, for despite the successes of native masters, it was still a vogue in London to favor the Continentals. Fuseli's *Nightmare* is a good example of the fantastic vision characteristic of much of his work. Some have even called him the father of the romantic movement in painting. Certainly one can detect something of the same horrid inspiration that haunted many of Goya's paintings and prints—which is no coincidence, for he had been schooled by Goya's master, Mengs.

Not even in the Renaissance did European art suffer so many shocks as it did in the nineteenth century, whose artistic chronicle is almost exclusively

ABOVE: ARAB CAVALIER, *BY EUGENE DELACROIX. (NEW YORK PUBLIC LIBRARY)*

OPPOSITE: JOCKEYS, *BY TOULOUSE-LAUTREC. (KNOEDLER GALLERIES, NEW YORK)*

confined to France. The era began with tremors produced by the French Revolution. Abruptly discarded were styles of art made popular by royal patronage. The new age belonged to the romantics, and the first of these to appear was the explosive Géricault, a master of horse painting. Ironically, this short-lived painter became infatuated with horses while in England. *Cavalry Officer Charging* (page 71), is one of the best recalled paintings. However, *A Horse* is perhaps the finest of his homages to that animal.

Géricault died in 1824, at the age of thirty-three. Delacroix was seven years his junior and destined to become the giant of the romantic painters. He was familiar with Géricault and, like the older man, he had visited Britain where he had been much taken with English tastes in sporting life, especially the hunt and the steeplechase. From both experiences he drew substantially for inspiration. But it was from literature, contemporary as well as classical, that Delacroix derived much subject matter (see page 209). In this chapter, we have a sketch, made during a visit to North

Africa, of an Arab Rider, full of the verve and nervous energy that mark Delacroix's notebooks and studies.

Manet is generally considered the painter whose vigor of style and violence of temperament prompted the birth of the Impressionist movement and who, in consequence, can be called the progenitor of modern painting. If one is surprised that Manet's painting should have occasioned so considerable a revulsion among the disciples of acceptable art in the middle of the nineteenth century, one must be even more startled to learn that a younger contemporary, Edgar Degas, inspired comparable outrage. Along with Delacroix and Géricault, Degas was a stellar painter of the horse who also succeeded in making splendid sculptural studies of the horse in motion—his achievements in that field unmatched since the time of Leonardo. His *Horse Walking* is an admirable demonstration of the artist's uncanny comprehension of the movements of the horse, and of the animal's grace and poise.

Another Impressionist who painted the horse in a new style was Pissarro, an old contemporary of Degas and represented here by his *Diligence at Louveciennes*. Once the dam of liberty had been breached, a flood of what most affluent or influential connoisseurs thought license flowed through the gap.

Of the many apostles of the late nineteenth-century movement called Post-Impressionism, Toulouse-Lautrec was one of the few to have had a serious personal and pleasurable interest in the horse; his *Jockeys* appears in this chapter. Other Post-Impressionist artists, such as Gauguin, made use of the horse —as in *White Horse*—for purely pictorial purposes having little or nothing

ABOVE: THE PADDOCK AT DEAUVILLE, *BY RAOUL DUFY. (CLICHÉ DES MUSÉES NATIONAUX)*

RIGHT: BLUE HORSES, BY FRANZ MARC. *(CLICHÉ DES MUSÉES NATIONAUX)*
OPPOSITE PAGE: GALLOPING HORSE, *BY EDVARD MUNCH (NATIONAL GALLERY, OSLO)*

206

to do with its virtuous attributes. As art became more and more expressive of private feelings and viewpoints, the "likeness to life" on which it had thrived for countless centuries ceased to matter very much.

The Austrian Franz Marc and the German Max Liebermann were precursors of a movement which was to be called Expressionism, a style that ultimately attracted many Germanic and Scandinavian artists of our own century, into which both men survived. Marc's *Blue Horses* and Liebermann's *Rider on the Beach* are both pictures of remarkable tranquillity for an age that was elsewhere producing works of such violence.

The phenomenon of art in the twentieth century is that it has proliferated, in almost every country of both hemispheres, in ways never before witnessed. Movements have not only succeeded one another with extraordinary rapidity but have frequently coincided, often headily. It is not possible to offer even a complete list of the "schools" of art that have blossomed and continued to bloom in one corner of the art world or another. It is not even useful to discuss the artists of a single country who have devoted some of their energies to the horse. For all but a few, however, the horse has served as a point of departure rather than as a creature to be honored for its own sake.

In this chapter are examples of horse-oriented art of the twentieth century by painters and sculptors whose careers span the entire period—artists who express as many different points of view as there are artists. They are natives of widely separated lands—though all countries are now connected by what André Malraux has described as the

"museum without walls," fine color reproductions of great art available to all at reasonable cost. Thus, for purposes of discussion, modern art is genuinely universal, with styles, techniques, tastes, and even markets confined to no single nation.

The Frenchman, Duchamp-Villon, who caused the artistic world of the United States to tremble in 1913 when his painting, *Nude Descending the Stairs*, was shown in New York and other American cities, produced in the following year a bronze sculpture of a horse's head, in which we may not be able to recognize many of the animal's traits. There is, all the same, a strong feeling of vitality and animation in the work, suggestive of the horse's characteristics.

The Norwegian Edvard Munch, one of the more powerful of the Expressionist painters and an emotionally disturbed personality, shows much of

OVERLEAF TOP: RIDER, 1951, BY MARINO MARINI. (PHOTO: CONZETT & HUBER, ZURICH)
MIDDLE: THE GENERALS, BY MARISOL, (ALBRIGHT-KNOX ART GALLERY, BUFFALO, GIFT OF SEYMOUR H. KNOX)
BOTTOM: HORSE, 1914, BY MARCEL DUCHAMPVILLON. (CLICHÉ DES MUSÉES NATIONAUX)
OPPOSITE PAGE: WAR, 1943, BY MARC CHAGALL. (CLICHÉ DES MUSÉES NATIONAUX)

his intensity in *The Galloping Horse*.

Rarely do we find pure geniality and charm in modern art. An enduring exception is the work of Raoul Dufy, a French painter and lithographer, who is often not thought sufficiently "serious" by contemporary critics who object to the presence of unmitigated pleasure in the art of their own time. Many of Dufy's paintings and prints illustrate the horse, and *The Paddock at Deauville* is a fine example of his beguiling manner in doing so.

The Russian-born Marc Chagall, a naturalized Frenchman like Picasso and Miró, has established his credentials as both a "serious" and amusing painter —and thus managed to elude the barbs of the most influential critics. One of his paintings, *War 1943*, is illustrated here. A master colorist like Dufy, Chagall is not so intent as the Frenchman on attaining a likeness to life. His interest seems to lie rather in the impact of an entire composition.

Marino Marini, the Italian sculptor, is obsessed with the horse to the exclusion of almost every other subject except, reasonably often, man as its rider. We do not presume to explain Marini's consuming passion. His horses evoke powerful feelings in the beholder, for they are extremely disturbing figures, their attitudes strange and not at all lifelike, their conformation bizarre. They are stunning, even alarming at times, but they cry more of humanity than of the horse.

We conclude with Marisol, the Venezuelan painter and sculptor, who has created the delightfully comic and enigmatic *Generals*, a pairing of George Washington and Napoleon on the barrel-shaped torso of a most improbable mount.

THE HORSE IN LITERATURE

THE HORSE, THE HORSE! THE SYMBOL OF SURGING POTENCY
AND POWER OF MOVEMENT, OF ACTION, IN MAN.
APOCALYPSE, D. H. LAWRENCE

There is not much doubt that more printed words have been dedicated to the horse than to any other living creature except, of course, man himself. It is not difficult to see why this should be so. On no other animal has man been so dependent for so long a period and for so many different reasons. The literature of the horse is analogous to the literature of history. That is, some of it is surpassingly beautiful, some touching, some downright silly as well as inaccurate. The difficulty that afflicts a high proportion of horselovers who undertake the praise or defense of the horse in print is similar to the one that disturbs the poet-lover; he loves unwisely and he does not write too well. He confuses feeling with sentimentality, pathos with bathos, and satire with burlesque.

Our concern in this chapter is with equine literature, not with instruction, with art rather than with craft. In the Appendix that follows are some selections that seem to me admirable less for their absolute fidelity to a set of facts than for their insights about man and the horse. It should be evident, however, that this is only a review of some striking pieces, not an anthology of the literature of the horse.

The Choice of a Horse

"In the choice of a horse and a wife, a man must please himself, ignoring the opinion and advice of friends." Thus did the nineteenth-century English writer, G. J. Whyte-Melville, summarize his position on this vital pair of subjects. He then proceeded to offer advice which, presumably, the man he had been referring to ought not to follow: "People talk about size, shape, quarters, blood, bone, muscle, but for my part give me a hunter with brains, he has to take care of the biggest fool of the two and think for both."

Whyte-Melville's key statement, of course, is that a man or woman (or child) must make a choice of animal

PRECEDING PAGE: DON QUIXOTE AND SANCHO PANZA, BY HONORÉ DAUMIER, CAPTURES AT ONCE THE HUMOR AND PATHOS OF DON QUIXOTE'S OBSESSION WITH CHIVALRY. (METROPOLITAN MUSEUM OF ART)

that is subjectively pleasing. "If the horse to be bought has already been ridden," counseled Xenophon, "we will give some directions which a man should observe who would escape being deceived in his purchase. First of all, he should know [the horse's] age. . . . Then, let it be observed how he bears the bit to be put into his mouth and the headpiece about his ears. . . . The next must be his behavior, when he receives his rider upon his back; for many horses will not submit, without difficulty, to bear such things to be done to them. . . ."

To be certain about the age of a horse is by no means an easy matter, and it has grown increasingly difficult as science has come to the assistance of the larcenous horse trader. The cultural antecedent of the used-car dealer, the horse trader, is a man who long ago grasped the essence of a successful transaction—the apparent bargain; that is, a means of conveyance that seems to be better than it really is. For every saying about the purchase of a car there is a counterpart about the purchase of a horse. At that point, however, the similarity ends, because the horse is animate. Once you have actually secured ownership of a horse, have ridden him or driven him, fed him and nurtured him, your emotions are in some fashion engaged. There are doubtless some car owners who enjoy similar feelings about a vehicle, but whether they concede the reality or not, such feelings are one-sided and limited.

It is these sentiments and sentimentalities that have produced equine literature of every variety, most of it inferior, some of it pretty competent, a bit of it truly wonderful. As we have seen, legend and mythology have greatly enhanced the horse's attributes, especially during

HORSES EXPRESS A LIMITED RANGE OF EMOTIONS, BUT OCCASIONALLY THEY DO COMMUNICATE SPECIFIC MOODS AND FEELINGS. (UNITED PRESS INTERNATIONAL)

213

the periods when only important or rich men and cavalry troopers were privileged to sit astride them. According to one of these legends, the celebrated Darius had to compete for the position of Persia's king against six other aspirants. When the seven rivals failed to agree on any rational way of choosing a leader, they resolved capriciously that he whose horse first uttered a sound should be awarded the crown. One may readily imagine the affection that Darius felt for his mount when it was the first to whinny. This improbable occurrence may have prompted Plutarch to give it as his view that "Nothing made the horse as fat as the king's eye." Darius' horse, if there is the slightest trace of truth in the tale, would have been made very fat indeed.

One of the first works of fiction to deal with the selection of a horse is Boccaccio's *Decameron*. In one of the stories, a man goes to Naples to purchase some horses. He loses his money and eventually replaces it by robbing the grave of a recently interred bishop. In another, the noble Francesco Vergellesi accepts from one Zima the gift of a magnificent horse in exchange for nothing more than permission to speak to Francesco's celebratedly chaste wife. The wife offers Zima no encouragement in his hot pursuit of her virtue. However, when her husband rides off to Milan on Zima's splendid stallion, she abruptly concludes that chastity is a very lonely way of reaching heaven. So she admits the lecherous Zima to her bed. Boccaccio would have us understand that Zima got the better of the bargain, but there is no record of Francesco's having been deceived by the horse he acquired.

Although literary opinions are very

FAUST AND MEPHISTOPHELES, BY EUGENE DELACROIX. NOTHING IN THE LEGEND OF FAUST'S SELLING HIS SOUL TO SATAN SUGGESTS THAT THEY NEGOTIATED WHILE ON HORSEBACK, BUT THE IDEA IS AN INTERESTING ONE. (METROPOLITAN MUSEUM OF ART, ROGERS FUND)

215

largely a matter of personal taste, and though many horselovers take the purchase of a horse so seriously that they shudder at the thought of levity in such a connection, my own view is that almost everything to be said on the subject is to be found in "Trinket's Colt," an early chapter of *Some Experiences of an Irish R. M.*, by O. E. E. Somerville and Martin Ross, two Anglo-Irish ladies who captured the rich flavor not merely of trafficking in horses but of human nature in Ireland around 1900. The excerpt appears in the Appendix.

The Possession of a Horse

The literature of Great Britain and the United States is cluttered with volumes devoted to the love of horses, and the quantity seems to have increased in more or less direct proportion to the decline of the animal's usefulness in both countries. There are some important nineteenth-century exceptions—*Black Beauty* is one. But in the main, it is in our own twentieth-century era that the horse has become a cynosure—very nearly an object of idolatry, particularly to the young, and most particularly to adolescent girls.

Certain psychologists have suggested that girls tend to lose their passionate interest in horses in proportion to their growing interest in boys. It is certainly true that there are many more youthful owners and riders and readers among girls, but the explanation may simply be that there are fewer outdoor sports available to girls than to boys. Riding is one of the sports, moreover, where girls may compete with members of the opposite sex on an equal basis. Indeed, in the Orwellian phrase, they are often more equal, for a competent woman is potentially a more valuable rider if she weighs less than an equally competent man.

The enormous quantity of juvenile literature dedicated to the horse is of very uneven quality. There has been some good fiction featuring horses, including entire series given over to numerous generations of them, notably the works of Marguerite Henry about the ponies of Chincoteague Island. Walter Farley has written an extended series of books, possibly the most popular ever composed on the horse. Engaging individual novels have appeared from time to time. Although they are ostensibly about horses, they are usually more about children or adolescents. *My Friend Flicka* and *National Velvet* are among the best known. *David Harum* is tangentially about horses, since the hero of that name was a redoubtable trader in horses. The western novel, the forerunner of the western movie, an art form that has become as stylized as the Elizabethan sonnet or Japanese haiku, was in the days of Zane Gray and Clarence

217

Mulford and Will James (to name but three of an awesome number of writers about the West), one of the most popular forms of literary entertainment for young and old in the United States and in Europe as well. The theme of the horse in the West has lost not one iota of its vitality or favor; it has simply shifted from the printed page to the screens of movies and television.

From the onset of recorded history, possession of a horse has always symbolized wealth, and to those whose lives or livelihood depended on this animal, its loss would be catastrophic. The horse in the days before the development of other means of transport was a vital piece of property, and much of common and statute law has been devoted to the protection of such property. To lose one's horse was not merely a matter of losing an item of property, however; it was to lose status, especially if the creature stolen were the only one the owner had title to. It meant that the loser had to walk, and to *have* to walk is to sacrifice one's dignity. Nor did it matter much what quality of animal was at issue. Well into this century, the stealing of a horse was a hanging offense in many parts of the world.

The horse as a status symbol in literature finds piquant expression in the figure of Rocinante, the mount of Don Quixote. There was scarcely a physical or moral complaint from which the poor creature did not suffer. Yet can you imagine the mad knight setting off to tilt at a windmill on foot? Sancho Panza, as befitted his inferior station, accompanied his master on the back of an ass, a creature, however, of much better health and a more comfortable ride than Rocinante. Yet Don Quixote thought himself the more suitably mounted merely

because Rocinante, whatever his short-comings, was a horse and not a donkey. And although he professed his death-less love for the chimerical Dulcinea, the possessed gentleman perceived in his horse an animal of fiery temperament and superb conformation. The fact was simple enough: Don Quixote was in love with his horse.

The absurdity of the knight's passion for Rocinante finds some echoes in the literature of other countries, but not often. Though other writers have touched on the theme occasionally, Cervantes' ludi-crous creation appears to be unique on the Continent, at any rate. The distinc-tion is noteworthy, for horse madness of the sort that produces a body of liter-ature seems to have been originally a British complaint, one that was brought to America by the English colonists of the early seventeenth century. In no other tongue do we find so many affec-tionate allusions to the horse. Is there, for instance, an equivalent in Russian or French or even American fiction of Squire Western in Fielding's *Tom Jones*, the most lovable fox-hunting man of all literature? Could you believe it of any-one but him that while in hottest pur-suit of his beloved daughter who had run away, he would pause long enough to follow a hunt across the countryside, for the reason that he could not love his dear Sophie half so much loved he not hunting more? "Mr. Western grew every day fonder and fonder of Sophia, inso-much that his beloved dogs themselves almost gave place to her in his affec-tions; but as he could not prevail on himself to abandon these, he contrived very cunningly to enjoy their company, together with that of his daughter, by insisting on her riding ahunting with him." We admit that Fielding exagger-

ates the case, that the headstrong squire is a gross caricature, yet he is immediately recognizable as an English country gentleman of the eighteenth century, for the simple reason that the author drew the portrait of Western straight from life. There are corners of Britain where his type still survives in oblivious comfort.

British horse madness is in part an accident of geography. There is not an authority anywhere who fails to agree that those islands off the west coast of Europe are the world's best possible breeding ground for horses. However, few city dwellers have developed a comparable affection for the cockroach just because the urban setting is ideal for that insect's proliferation. It was more than merely the lush grasslands and a climate without severe extremes of heat or cold that occasioned this curious, almost exclusively British addiction. It was also the possibility of idleness that existed for the upper class, the result of a long period of mercantile expansion that produced a constantly increasing balance of payments. It was

also a singular island setting that made the country proof against serious threat of attack from abroad. Defense, therefore, required no great or consistent effort. As a matter of fact, no effort of any sort was asked or expected of most gentlemen.

This spirit of idleness that still informs a significant number of English and Irish country gentlemen is frequently misunderstood by foreigners. The principle decrees not that a gentleman do nothing, but that he do nothing of importance. Hence, the British gentry's extraordinary affection for cricket. the most leisurely-paced sport ever devised. Hence, fox-hunting—"the unspeakable in full pursuit of the uneatable," as the Irish Oscar Wilde characterized the typical activity of the English country gentleman. Here is a pastime that involves as many as forty hounds and frequently more than a hundred riders. A particularly strenuous hunt may occupy all the daylight of every day during the various seasons. To the devoted fox or stag hunter it is a passion as consuming as the love for woman or for God.

Of nineteenth-century English chroniclers of the hunt, one of the most cherished by the British themselves is R. S. Surtees, creator of Jorrocks, the archetypal follower of the hounds. When compared with the delicacy and acuity of Somerville and Ross, however, Surtees' gross "jollities" appear forced. In quite another vein is Lord Byron's poem, "Mazeppa," the saga of a Polish nobleman whose life was saved by a Ukrainian wild horse, quite the finest of the enormous range of nineteenth-century poetry involving the horse.

Siegfried Sassoon, member of a prominent English family of bankers, succeed-

220

222

ed, in *Memoirs of a Fox-Hunting Man*, to convey the combination of excitement, sense of possible danger, love of the outdoors, and the pleasure of riding a competent horse that are the essence of the sport. The description of his very first hunt appears in the Appendix.

It is scarcely to be wondered at that when the greatest Irish genius of dazzling after-dinner conversation, which he composed in the form of plays, George Bernard Shaw, came to grips with the British and their madness of the hunt, he should have treated it with devastating sarcasm. The following is extracted from a speech in *Heartbreak House*:

. . . Why have we never been able to let this house? Because there are no proper stables. Go anywhere in England where there are natural, wholesome, contented, and really nice English people; and what do you always find? That the stables are the real centre of the household; and that if any visitor wants to play the piano the whole room has to be upset before it can be opened, there are so many things piled on it. I never lived until I learned to ride; and I shall never ride really well because I didn't begin as a child. There are only two classes of good society in England; the equestrian classes and the neurotic classes. It isn't mere convention; everybody can see that the people who hunt are the right people and the people who don't are the wrong ones.

Shavian playfulness and caricature are only slight distortions of utter reality. Squire Western, had he cared about "right" people and "wrong" people, could very naturally have uttered the words which Shaw put into the mouth of Lady Utterwood.

Interpreting the actions and attitudes of animals as though they were human beings is a frequent and mainly abominable literary device. *Black Beauty*, in which the narrator pretends to be a horse, is probably the most celebrated and exasperating example of such anthropomorphism. The basic difficulty is that when a writer tries to imagine what it is like to be an animal, he tends to ascribe to the beast the emotions and intellectual processes of man. The result can only be spurious.

On the other hand, there have been some amusing works in which the spirit of man has been transmuted, for one reason or another, to the body of a donkey. Two examples that leap to mind are *The Golden Ass* and *A Midsummer Night's Dream*. In both instances, the writer treats the donkey as a figure of fun. Perhaps the horse has

LEFT: RICHARD II CAPTURED BY BOLINGBROKE, *FROM A MEDIEVAL ILLUMINATED MANUSCRIPT.* (BRITISH MUSEUM)
RIGHT: *ON THIS PLATE OF ABOUT 1680 BY THOMAS TOFT, CHARLES II IS DEPICTED IN A TREE, BESET BY A MANTICORE AND A UNICORN, BOTH HERALDIC SYMBOLS.* (METROPOLITAN MUSEUM OF ART)

223

not been so dealt with because its beauty and value are too deeply impressed upon the common consciousness to allow it to be the object of jest.

The Horse as Conveyance

Medieval chivalry was a way of life linked by tradition to the earlier era of Charlemagne and celebrated in such tales as the *Roman de la Rose*, the *Chanson de Roland*, the Arthurian tales, and the Spanish accounts of El Cid. In all of these epics, as in the folklore of the Teutons and the Scandinavians, the horse played an important role. With the First Crusade to wrest possession of the holy places of Palestine from Islam, the mounted knight rode out of legend into the light of historical fact.

In general, the best writing about the horse has been devoted to his capacity to carry people and to pull their vehicles, especially under difficult conditions. Every historian has paid homage, if only in passing, to the role of the horse in errands of peace, mercy, and war. Of course, in all these instances, it is man who has been aided, not other horses. We should probably not complain about this. If the horse appears most frequently as subservient to man, so does virtually every other force and creature. It is a small price to pay for lines by Shakespeare. The horse figures in so many of his plays that one hardly knows from which to choose for quotation. Two passages do, nevertheless, seem to stand out, contrasting dramatically with each other in matter and manner, yet both having to do with the horse as convenience and conveyance. The first is from *Henry the Fifth*, the second from *The Taming of the Shrew*. Both appear in the Appendix.

American writers have contributed handsomely to the literature of the horse. John Steinbeck's *The Red Pony* may be the finest example composed in this century. But it is impossible to propose any text than can be fairly juxtaposed to Shakespeare's. Consequently, we conclude with a piece of verbal slapstick about the harnessing of a horse, European style, from *The Innocents Abroad*, by Mark Twain:

It may interest the reader to know how they "put horses to" on the continent. The man stands up the horses on each side of the thing that projects from the front end of the wagon, and then throws the tangled mess of gear on top of the horses, and passes the thing that goes forward through a ring, and hands if aft, and passes the other thing through the other ring and hands it aft on the other side of the other horse, opposite to the first one, after crossing them and bringing the loose end back, and then buckles the other thing underneath the horse, and takes another thing and wraps it around the thing I spoke of before, and puts another thing over each horse's head, with broad flappers to keep the dust out of his eyes, and puts the iron thing in his mouth for him to grit his teeth on, up hill, and brings the ends of these things after over his back, after buckling another one under his neck to hold his head up, and hitching another thing on a thing that goes over his shoulders to keep his head up when he is climbing a hill, and then takes the slack of the thing which I mentioned a while ago, and fetches it aft and makes it fast to the thing that pulls the wagon, and hands the other thing up to the driver to steer with. I have never buckled up a horse myself, but I do not think we do it that way.

Appendix

The Horse in Literature: A small sampling

From "The Taming of the Shrew," by Shakespeare. Biondello describes the arrival of Petruchio before the house of Batista, to claim the hand of his headstrong daughter, Katharina.

Why, Petruchio is coming in a new hat and an old jerkin; a pair of old breeches thrice turned; a pair of boots that have been candle cases, one buckled, another laced; an old rusty sword ta'en out of the town armory, with a broken hilt, and chapeless; with two broken points; his horse hipped with an old mothy saddle, and stirrups of no kindred, besides, possessed with the glanders and like to mose in the chine, troubled with the lampass, infected with the fashions, full of windgalls, sped with spavins, rayed with the yellows, past cure of the fives, stark spoiled with the staggers, begnawn with the bots, swayed in the back and shoulder-shotten, near-legged before and with a half-cheeked bit and a headstall of sheep's leather which, being restrained to keep him from stumbling, hath been often burst and now repaired with knots, one girth six times pieced, and a woman's crupper of velure which hath two letters for her name fairly set down in studs and here and there pieced with pack thread.

From "Gulliver's Travels," by Jonathan Swift

But looking on my left hand, I saw a horse walking softly in the field; which my persecutors having sooner discovered, was the cause of their flight. The horse started a little when he came near me, but soon recovering himself, looked full in my face with manifest tokens of wonder: he viewed my hands and feet, walking round me several times. I would have pursued my journey, but he placed himself directly in the way, yet looking with a very mild aspect, never offering the least violence. We stood gazing at each other for some time; at last, I took the boldness to reach my hand towards his neck, with a design to stroak it; using the common style and whistles of jockies when they are going to handle a strange horse. But, this animal seeming to receive my civilities with disdain, shook his head, and bent his brows, softly raising up his left fore foot to remove my hand. Then he neighed three or four times, but in so different a cadence, that I almost began to think he was speaking to himself in some language of his own.

While he and I were thus employed, another horse came up; who applying himself to the first in a very formal manner, they gently struck each others right hoof before, neighing several times by turns, and varying the sound, which seemed to be almost articulate. They went off some paces, as if it were to confer together, walking side by side, backward and forward, like persons deliberating some affair of weight; but often turning their eyes towards me,

225

as it were to watch that I might not escape. I was amazed to see such actions and behaviour in brute beasts; and concluded with myself, that if the inhabitants of this country were endued with a proportionable degree of reason, they must needs be the wisest people upon earth. This thought gave me so much comfort, that I resolved to go forward until I could discover some house or village, or meet with any of the natives, leaving the two horses to discourse together as they pleased. But the first, who was a dapple-grey, observing me to steal off, neighed after me in so expressive a tone, that I fancied myself to understand what he meant; whereupon I turned back, and came near him, to expect his further commands; but concealing my fear as much as I could, for I began to be in some pain, how this adventure might terminate; and the reader will easily believe, I did not much like my present situation.

The two horses came up close to me, looking with great earnestness upon my face and hands. The grey steed rubbed my hat all round with his right fore hoof, and discomposed it so much, that I was forced to adjust it better, by taking it off, and settling it again; whereat both he and his companion, (who was a brown bay) appeared to be much surprised; the latter felt the lappet of my coat, and finding it to hang loose about me, they both looked with new signs of wonder. He stroked my right hand, seeming to admire the softness, the colour; but he squeezed it so hard between

his hoof and pastern, that I was forced to roar; after which they both touched me with all possible tenderness. They were under great perplexity about my shoes and stockings, which they felt very often, neighing to each other, and using various gestures, not unlike those of a philosopher, when he would attempt to solve some new and difficult phaenomenon.

Upon the whole, the behaviour of these animals was so orderly and rational, so acute and judicious, that I at last concluded, they must needs be magicians, who had thus metamorphosed themselves upon some design; and seeing a stranger in the way, were resolved to divert themselves with him; or perhaps were really amazed at the sight of a man so very different in habit, feature and complexion from those who might probably live in so remote a climate. Upon the strength of this reasoning, I ventured to address them in the following manner: "Gentlemen, if you be conjurers, as I have good cause to believe, you can understand any language; therefore I make bold to let your worships know, that I am a poor distressed Englishman, driven by his misfortunes upon your coast; and I entreat one of you to let me ride upon his back, as if he were a real horse, to some house or village, where I can be relieved. In return of which favour, I will make you a present of this knife and bracelet" (taking them out of my pocket). The two creatures stood silent while I spoke, seeming to listen with great attention; and when I had ended, they

neighed frequently towards each other, as if they were engaged in serious conversation. I plainly observed, that their language expressed the passions very well, and the words might with little pain be resolved into an alphabet more easily than the Chinese.

"Trinket's Colt," from "Some Experiences of an Irish R. M." by OE. E. Somerville and Martin Ross[1]

It was Petty Sessions Day in Skebawn, a cold, grey day of February. A case of trespass had dragged its burden of cross summonses and cross swearings far into the afternoon, and when I left the bench my head was singing from the bellowings of the attorneys, and the smell of their clients was heavy upon my palate.

The streets still testified to the fact that it was market day, and I evaded with difficulty the sinuous course of soddenly screwed people, and steered an equally devious one for myself among the groups anchored round the doors of the public-houses. Skebawn possesses, among its legion of public-houses, one establishment which timorously, and almost imperceptibly, proffers tea to the thirsty. I turned in there, as was my custom on court days, and found the dingy little den, known as the Ladies' Coffee-Room, in the occupancy of my friend Mr. Florence McCarthy Knox, who was drinking strong tea and eating buns with serious simplicity. It was a first and quite unexpected glimpse of that domesticity that has now become a marked feature of his character.

"You're the very man I wanted to see," I said as I sat down beside him at the oilcloth-covered table; "a man I know in England who is not much of a judge of character has asked me to buy him a four-year-old down here, and as I should rather be stuck by a friend than a dealer, I wish you'd take over the job."

Flurry poured himself out another cup of tea, and dropped three lumps of sugar into it in silence.

Finally he said, "There isn't a four-year-old in this country that I'd be seen dead with at a pig fair."

This was discouraging, from the premier authority on horse-flesh in the district.

"But it isn't six weeks since you told me you had the finest filly in your stable that was ever foaled in the County Cork," I protested; "what's wrong with her?"

"Oh, is it that filly?" said Mr. Knox with a lenient smile; "she's gone these three weeks from me. I swapped her and £6 for a three-year-old Ironmonger colt, and after that I swapped the colt and £19 for that Bandon horse I rode last week at your place, and after that again I sold the Bandon horse for £75 to old Welply, and I had to give him back a couple of sovereigns luck-money. You see I did pretty well with that filly after all."

"Yes, yes—oh rather," I assented, as one dizzily accepts the propositions of the bimetallist; "and you don't know of anything else—?"

The room in which we were seated was closely screened from the shop by a door with a muslin-curtained window in it; several of the panes were broken, and at this juncture two voices that had for some time carried on a discussion forced themselves upon our attention.

"Begging your pardon for contradicting you, ma'am," said the voice of Mrs. McDonald, proprietress of the teashop, and a leading light in Skebawn Dissenting circles, shrilly tremulous with indignation, "if the servants I recommend to you won't stop with you, it's no fault of mine. If respectable girls are set picking grass out of your gravel, in place of their proper work, certainly they will give you warning!"

The voice that replied struck me as being a notable one, well bred and imperious.

"When I take a barefooted slut out of a cabin, I don't expect her to dictate to me what her duties are!"

Flurry jerked up his chin in a noiseless laugh. "It's my grandmother!" he whispered. "I bet you Mrs. McDonald don't get much change out of her!"

"If I set her to clean the pig-sty I expect her to obey me," continued the voice in accents that would have made me clean forty pigsties had she desired me to do so.

"Very well, ma'am," retorted Mrs. McDonald, "if that's the way you treat your servants, you needn't come here again looking for them. I consider your conduct neither that of a lady nor a Christian!"

"Don't you, indeed?" replied

Flurry's grandmother. "Well, your opinion doesn't greatly disturb me, for, to tell you the truth, I don't think you're much of a judge."

"Didn't I tell you she'd score?" murmured Flurry, who was by this time applying his eye to a hole in the muslin curtain. "She's off," he went on, returning to his tea. "She's a great character! She's eighty-three if she's a day, and she's as sound on her legs as a three-year-old! Did you see that old shandrydan of hers in the street a while ago, and a fellow on the box with a red beard on him like Robinson Crusoe? That old mare on the near side—Trinket is her name—is mighty near clean bred. I can tell you her foals are worth a bit of money."

I had heard of Mrs. Knox of Aussolas; indeed, I had seldom dined out in the neighborhood without hearing some new story about her and her remarkable ménage, but it had not yet been my privilege to meet her.

227

"Well, now," went on Flurry in his slow voice, "I'll tell you a thing that's just come into my head. My grandmother promised me a foal of Trinket's the day I was one-and-twenty, and that's five years ago, and deuce a one I've got from her yet. You never were at Aussolas? No, you were not. Well, I tell you the place there is like a circus with horses. She has a couple of score of them running wild in the woods, like deer."

"Oh, come," I said, "I'm a bit of a liar myself—"

"Well, she has a dozen of them anyhow, rattling good colts, too, some of them, but they may as well be donkeys for all the good they are to me or anyone. It's not once in three years she sells one, and there she has them walking after her for bits of sugar, like a lot of dirty lapdogs," ended Flurry with disgust.

"Well, what's your plan? Do you want me to make a bid for one of her lapdogs?"

"I was thinking," replied Flurry, with great deliberation, "that my birthday's this week, and maybe I would work a four-year-old of Trinket's she has out of her in honour of the occasion."

"And sell your grandmother's birthday present to me?"

"Just that, I suppose," answered Flurry, with a slow wink.

A few days afterwards a letter from Mr. Knox informed me that he had "squared the old lady, and it would be all right about the colt." He further told me that Mrs. Knox had been good enough to offer me, with him, a day's snipe shooting on the celebrated Aussolas bogs, and he proposed to drive me there the following Monday, if convenient. Most people found it convenient to shoot the Aussolas snipe bog when they got the chance. Eight o'clock on the following Monday morning saw Flurry, myself, and a groom packed into a dogcart, with portmanteaus, gun-cases, and two rampant red setters.

It was a long drive, twelve miles at least, and a very cold one. We passed through long tracts of pasture country, fraught, for Flurry, with memories of runs, which were recorded for me, fence by fence, in every one of which the biggest dog-fox in the country had gone to ground, with not two feet—measured accurately by the handle of the whip—between him and the leading hound; through bogs that imperceptibly melted into lakes, and finally down and down into a valley, where the fir-trees of Aussolas clustered darkly round a glittering lake, and all but hid the grey roofs and pointed gables of Aussolas Castle.

"There's a nice stretch of demesne for you," remarked Flurry, pointing downwards with a whip, "and one little old woman holding it all in the heel of her fist. Well able to hold it she is, and always was, and she'll live twenty years yet, if it's only to spite us, and when all's said and done goodness knows how she'll leave it!"

"It strikes me you were lucky to keep her to her promise about the colt," I said.

Flurry administered a composing kick to the ceaseless strivings of the red setters under the seat.

"I used to be rather a pet with her," he said, after a pause; "but mind you, I haven't got him yet, and if she gets any notion I want to sell him I'll never get him, so say nothing about the business to her."

The tall gates of Aussolas shrieked on their hinges as they admitted us, and shut with a clang behind us, in the faces of an old mare and a couple of young horses, who, foiled in their break for the excitements of the outer world, turned and galloped defiantly on either side of us. Flurry's admirable cob hammered on, regardless of all things save his duty.

"He's the only one that I'd trust myself with here," said his master, flicking him approvingly with the whip; "there are plenty of people afraid to come here at all, and when my grandmother goes out driving she has a boy on the box with a basket full of stones to peg at them. Talk of the dickens, here she is herself!"

A short, upright old woman was approaching, preceded by a white woolly dog with sore eyes and a bark like a tin trumpet; we both got out of the trap and advanced to meet the lady of the manor.

I may summarize her attire by saying that she looked as if she had robbed a scarecrow; her face was small and incongruously refined, the skinny hand that she extended to me had the grubby tan that bespoke the professional gardener, and was decorated with a magnificent diamond ring. On her head was a massive purple bonnet.

"I am very glad to meet you,

Major Yeates," she said with an old-fashioned precision of utterance; "your grandfather was a dancing partner of mine in the old days at the Castle [Dublin Castle, seat of Britain's government in Ireland], when he was a handsome young aide-de-camp, and I was —You may judge for yourself what I was."

She ended with a startling little hoot of laughter, and I was aware that she quite realized the world's opinion of her, and was indifferent to it.

Our way to the bogs took us across Mrs. Knox's home farm, and through a large field in which several young horses were grazing.

"There now, that's my fellow," said Flurry, pointing to a fine-looking colt, "the chestnut with the white diamond on his forehead. He'll run into three figures before he's done, but we'll not tell that to the old lady!"

The famous Aussolas bogs were as full of snipe as usual, and a good deal fuller of water than any bogs I had ever shot before. I was on my day, and Flurry was not, and as he is ordinarily an infinitely better snipe shot than I, I felt at peace with the world and all men as we walked back, wet through, at five o'clock.

The sunset had waned, and a big white moon was making the eastern tower of Aussolas look like a thing in a fairy tale or a play when we arrived at the hall door. An individual, whom I recognized as the Robinson Crusoe coachman, admitted us to a hall, the like of which one does not often see. The

walls were panelled with dark oak up to the gallery that ran round three sides of it, the balusters of the wide staircase were heavily carved, and blackened portraits of Flurry's ancestors on the spindle side stared sourly down on their descendant as he tramped upstairs with the bog mould on his hobnailed boots.

We had just changed into dry clothes when Robinson Crusoe showed his red beard round the corner of the door, with the information that his mistress said we were to stay for dinner. My heart sank. It was then barely half-past five. I said something about having no evening clothes and having to get home early.

"Sure the dinner'll be in another half-hour," said Robinson Crusoe, joining hospitably in the conversation; "and as for evening clothes —God bless ye!"

The door closed behind him.

"Never mind," said Flurry, "I dare say you'll be glad enough to eat another dinner by the time you get home." He laughed. "Poor Slipper!" he added inconsequentially, and only laughed again when I asked him for an explanation.

Old Mrs. Knox received us in the library, where she was seated by a roaring turf fire, which lit the room a good deal more effectively than the pair of candles that stood beside her in tall silver candlesticks. Ceaseless and implacable growls indicated the presence of the woolly dog. She talked with confounding culture of the books that rose all round her to the ceiling; her evening dress was accom-

plished by means of an additional white shawl, rather dirtier than its congeners; as I took her into dinner she quoted Virgil to me, and in the same breath she screeched an objurgation at a being whose matted hair rose suddenly into view from behind an ancient Chinese screen, as I have seen the head of a Zulu woman peer over a bush.

Dinner was as incongruous as everything else. Detestable soup in a splendid old silver tureen that was nearly as dark in hue as Robinson Crusoe's thumb; a perfect salmon, perfectly cooked, on a chipped kitchen dish; such cut glass as is not easy to find nowadays; a sherry that, as Flurry subsequently remarked, would burn the shell off an egg; a bottle of port, draped in immemorial cobwebs, wan with age, and probably priceless. Throughout the vicissitudes of the meal Mrs. Knox's conversation flowed on undismayed, directed sometimes at me—she had installed me in the position of friend of her youth, and she talked to me as if I were my own grandfather—sometimes at Crusoe, with whom she had several heated arguments, and sometimes she would make a statement of remarkable frankness on the subject of her horse-farming affairs to Flurry, who, very much on his best behaviour, agreed with all she said, and risked no original remark. As I listened to them both, I remembered with infinite amusement how he had told me once that "a pet name she had for him was 'Tony Lumpkin,' and no one but herself knew what she meant by it." It seemed strange that she made no allusion to Trinket's colt or to Flurry's birthday, but, mindful of my instructions, I held my peace.

As, at about half-past eight, we drove away in the moonlight, Flurry congratulated me solemnly on my success with his grandmother. He was good enough to tell me that she would marry me to-morrow if I asked her, and he wished I would, even if it was only to see what a nice grandson he'd be for me. A sympathetic giggle behind me told me that Michael, on the back seat, had heard and relished the jest.

We had left the gates of Aussolas about a half a mile behind when, at the corner of a by-road, Flurry pulled up. A short squat figure arose from the black shadow of a furze bush and came into the moonlight, swinging its arms like a cabman and cursing audibly.

"Oh murdher, oh murdher, Misther Flurry! What kept ye at all? 'Twould perish the crows to be wasting here the way I am these two hours—"

"Ah, shut your mouth, Slipper!" said Flurry, who, to my surprise, had turned back the rug and was taking off his driving coat, "I couldn't help it. Come on, Yeates, we've got to get out of here."

"What for?" I asked, in not unnatural bewilderment.

"It's all right. I'll tell you as we go along," replied my companion, who was already turning to follow Slipper up the by-road. "Take the trap on, Michael, and wait at the River's Cross." He waited for me to come up with him, and then put his hand on my arm. "You see, Major, this is the way it is. My grandmother's given me that colt right enough, but if I waited for her to send him over I'd never see a hair of his tail. So I just thought that as we were over here we might as well take him back with us, and maybe you'll give us a help with him; he'll not be altogether too handy for a first go-off."

I was staggered. An infant in arms could scarcely have failed to discern the fishiness of the transaction, and I begged Mr. Knox not to put himself to this trouble on my account, as I had no doubt I could find a horse for my friend elsewhere. Mr. Knox assured me that it was no trouble at all, quite the contrary, and that, since his grandmother had given him the colt, he saw no reason why he should not take him when he wanted him; also, that if I didn't want him he'd be glad enough to keep him himself; and finally, that I wasn't the chap to go back on a friend, but I was welcome to drive back to Shreelane with Michael this minute if I liked.

Of course I yielded in the end. I told Flurry I should lose my job over the business, and he said I could marry his grandmother, and the discussion was abruptly closed by the necessity of following Slipper over a locked five-barred gate.

Our pioneer took us over about half a mile of country, knocking down stone gaps where practicable and scrambling over tall banks in the deceptive moonlight. We found ourselves at length in a field with a shed in one corner of it; in a dim group of buildings a little way off a light was shining.

"Wait here," said Flurry to me in a whisper; "the less noise the better. It's an open shed, and we'll just slip in and coax him out."

Slipper unwound from his waist a halter, and my colleagues glided like spectres into the shadow of the shed, leaving me to meditate on my duties as Resident Magistrate, and on the questions that would be asked in the House [Commons] by our local member when Slipper had given away the adventure in his cups.

In less than a minute three shadows emerged from the shed, where two had gone in. They had the colt. "He came out as quiet as a calf when he winded the sugar," said Flurry; "it was well for me I filled my pockets from grandmamma's sugar-basin."

He and Slipper had a rope from each side of the colt's head; they took him quickly across a field towards a gate. The colt stepped daintily between them over the

230

moonlit grass; he snorted occasionally, but appeared on the whole amenable.

The trouble began later, and was due, as trouble often is, to the beguilements of a short cut. Against the maturer judgement of Slipper, Flurry insisted on following a route that he assured us he knew as well as his own pocket, and the consequence was that in about five minutes I found myself standing on top of a bank hanging on to a rope, on the other end of which the colt dangled and dance, while Flurry, with the other rope, lay prone in the ditch, and Slipper administered to the bewildered colt's hindquarters such chastisements as could be ventured on.

I have no space to narrate in detail the atrocious difficulties and disasters of the short cut. How the colt set to work to buck, and went away across a field, dragging the faithful Slipper literally *ventre-à-terre*, after him, while I picked myself in ignominy out of a briar patch, and Flurry cursed himself black in the face. How we were attacked by ferocious cur dogs, and I lost my eye-glass; and how, as we neared the River's Cross, Flurry espied the police patrol on the road, and we all hid behind a rick of turf, while I realized in fullness what an exceptional ass I was, to have been beguiled into an enterprise that involved hiding with Slipper from the Royal Irish Constabulary!

Let it suffice to say that Trinket's infernal offspring was finally handed over on the high-road to Michael and Slipper, and Flurry

drove me home in a state of mental and physical overthrow.

I saw nothing of my friend Mr. Knox for the next couple of days, by the end of which time I had worked up a high polish on my misgivings, and had determined to tell him that under no circumstances would I have anything to say to his grandmother's birthday present. It was like my usual luck that, instead of writing a note to this effect, I thought it would be good for my liver to walk across the hills to Tory Cottage and tell Flurry so in person.

It was a bright, blustery morning, after a muggy day. The feeling of spring was in the air, the daffodils were already in bud, and crocuses showed purple in the grass on either side of the avenue. It was only a couple of miles to Tory Cottage across the hills; I walked fast, and it was barely twelve o'clock when I saw its pink walls and clumps of evergreen below me. As I looked down at it the chiming of Flurry's hounds in the kennels came to me on the wind; I stood still to listen, and could almost have sworn that I was hearing again the clash of Magdalen [College] bells, hard at work on May morning.

The path that I was following led downwards through a larch plantation to Flurry's back gate. Hot wafts from some hideous caldron at the other side of a wall apprised me of the vicinity of the kennels and their cuisine, and the fir-trees round were hung with gruesome and unknown joints. I thanked Heaven that I was not

master of hounds, and passed on as quickly as might be to the hall door.

I rang two or three times without response; then the door opened a couple of inches and was instantly slammed in my face. I heard the hurried padding of bare feet on oilcloth, and a voice, "Hurry, Bridgie, hurry! There's quality at the door!"

Bridgie, holding a dirty cap on with one hand, presently arrived and informed me that she believed Mr. Knox was about the place. She seemed perturbed, and she cast scared glances down the drive while speaking to me.

I knew enough of Flurry's habits to shape a tolerably direct course for his whereabouts. He was, as I had expected, in the training paddock, a field behind the stable-yard, in which he had put up practice jumps for his horses. It was a good-sized field with clumps of furze in it, and Flurry was standing near one of these with his hands in

231

his pockets, singularly unoccupied. I supposed that he was prospecting for a place to put up another jump. He did not see me coming, and turned with a start as I spoke to him. There was a queer expression of mingled guilt and what I can only describe as divilment in his grey eyes as he greeted me. In my dealing with Flurry Knox, I have since formed the habit of sitting tight, in a general way, when I see that expression.

"Well, who's coming next, I wonder!" he said, as he shook hands with me; "it's not ten minutes since I had two of your d----d peelers searching the whole place for my grandmother's colt!"

"What!" I exclaimed, feeling the cold all down my back; "do you mean the police have got hold of it?"

"They haven't got hold of the colt anyway," said Flurry, looking sideways at me from under the peak of his cap, with the glint of the sun in his eye. "I got word in time before they came."

"What do you mean?" I demanded; "where is he? For Heaven's sake don't tell me you've sent the brute over to my place!"

"It's a good job for you I didn't," replied Flurry, "as the police are on their way to Shreelane this minute to consult you about it. *You!*" He gave utterance to one of his short diabolical fits of laughter. "He's where they'll not find him, anyhow. Ho! ho! It's the funniest hand I ever played!"

"Oh yes, it's devilish funny, I've no doubt," I retorted, beginning to lose my temper, as is the manner

of many people when they are frightened; "but I give you fair warning that if Mrs. Knox asks me any questions about it, I shall tell her the whole story."

"All right," responded Flurry; "and when you do, don't forget to tell her how you flogged the colt on to the road over her own bounds ditch."

"Very well," I said hotly, "I may as well go home and send in my papers. They'll break me over this—"

"Ah, hold on, Major," said Flurry soothingly, "It'll be all right. No one knows anything. It's only on spec the old lady sent the bobbies here. If you'll keep quiet it'll all blow over."

"I don't care," I said, struggling hopelessly in the toils; "if I meet your grandmother, and she asks me about it, I shall tell her all I know."

"Please God you'll not meet her! After all, it's not once in a blue moon that she—" began Flurry. Even as he said the words his face changed. "Holy fly!" he ejaculated, "isn't that her dog coming into the field? Look at her bonnet over the wall! Hide, hide for your life!" He caught me by the shoulders and shoved me down among the furze bushes before I realized what had happened.

"Get in there! I'll talk to her."

I may as well confess that at the mere sight of Mrs. Knox's purple bonnet my heart turned to water. In that moment I knew what it would be like to tell her how I, having eaten her salmon, and capped her quotations, and drunk her best port, had gone forth and helped to steal her horse. I aban-

doned my dignity, my sense of honour; I took the furze prickles to my breast and wallowed in them.

Mrs. Knox advanced with vengeful speed; already she was in high altercation with Flurry at no great distance from where I lay; varying sounds of battle reached me, and I gathered that Flurry was not—to put it mildly—shrinking from that economy of the truth that the situation demanded.

"Is it that curby, long-backed brute? You promised him to me long ago, but I wouldn't be bothered with him!"

The old lady uttered a laugh of shrill derision. "Is it likely that I'd promise you my best colt? And still more, is it likely you'd refuse him if I did?"

"Very well, ma'am," Flurry's voice was admirably indignant. "Then I suppose I'm a liar and a thief."

"I'd be more obliged to you for the information if I hadn't known it before," responded his grandmother with lightning speed; "if you swore to me on a stack of bibles you knew nothing about my colt I wouldn't believe you! I shall go straight to Major Yeates and ask his advice. I believe *him* to be a gentleman, in spite of the company he keeps!"

I writhed deeper in the furze bushes, and thereby discovered a sandy rabbit run, along which I crawled, with my cap well down over my eyes, and the furze needles stabbing me through my stockings. The ground shelved a little, promising profounder concealment, but the bushes were very thick, and I laid hold of the bare stem of one to help my progress. It lifted out of the ground in my hand, revealing a freshly cut stump. Something snorted, not a yard away; I glared through the opening, and was confronted by the long, horrified face of Mrs. Knox's colt, mysteriously on a level with my own.

Even without the white diamond on his forehead, I should have divined the truth; but how in the name of wonder had Flurry persuaded him to couch like a woodcock in the heart of a furze brake? For a full minute I lay as still as death for fear of frightening him, while the voices of Flurry and his grandmother raged on alarmingly close to me. The colt snorted, and blew long breaths through his wide nostrils, but he did not move. I crawled an inch or two nearer, and after a few seconds of cautious peering I grasped the position. They had buried him.

A small sandpit among the furze had been utilized as a grave; they had filled him in up to his withers with sand, and a few furze bushes, artistically disposed round the pit, had done the rest. As the depth of Flurry's guile was revealed, laughter came upon me like a flood; I gurgled and shook apoplectically, and the colt gazed at me with serious surprise, until a sudden outburst of barking close to my elbow administered a fresh shock to my tottering nerves.

Mrs. Knox's woolly dog had tracked me into the furze, and was now baying the colt and me with mingled terror and indignation. I addressed him with a whisper, with perfidious endearments, advancing a crafty hand towards him the while, made a snatch for the back of his neck, missed it badly, and got hold of him by the ragged fleece of his hind-quarters as he tried to flee. If I had flayed him alive he would hardly have uttered a more deafening series of yells, but, like a fool, instead of letting him go, I dragged him towards me, and tried to stifle the noise by holding his muzzle. The tussle lasted engrossingly for a few seconds, and then the climax of the nightmare arrived.

Mrs. Knox's voice, close behind me, said, "Let go of my dog this instant, sir! Who are you—"

Her voice faded away, and I knew that she had seen the colt's head.

I felt positively sorry for her. At her age there was no knowing what effect the shock might have on her. I scrambled to my feet and confronted her.

"Major Yeates!" she said. There was a deathly pause. "Will you kindly tell me," said Mrs. Knox slowly, "am I in Bedlam, or are you? And *what is that?*"

She pointed to the colt, and that unfortunate animal, recognizing the voice of his mistress, uttered a hoarse and lamentable whinny. Mrs. Knox felt around her for support, found only furze prickles, gazed speechlessly at me, and then, to her eternal honour, fell into wild cackles of laughter.

So, I may say, did Flurry and I. I embarked on my explanations and broke down; Flurry followed suit and broke down too. Over-

whelming laughter held us all three, disintegrating our very souls. Mrs. Knox pulled herself together first.

"I acquit you, Major Yeates, I acquit you, though appearances are against you. It's clear enough to me that you've fallen among thieves." She stopped and glowered at Flurry. Her purple bonnet was over one eye. "I'll thank you, sir," she said, "to dig out that horse before I leave this place. And when you've dug him out you may keep him. I'll be no receiver of stolen goods."

She broke off and shook her fist at him. "Upon my conscience, Tony, I'd give a guinea to have thought of it myself!"

From "Memoirs of a Fox-Hunting Man," by Siegfried Sassoon[2]

It was a grey and chilly world that I went out into when I started for my first day's fox-hunting. The winter-smelling air met me as though with a hint that serious events were afoot. Silently I stood in the stable-yard while Dixon led Sheila out of her stall. Her demeanour was businesslike and reticent. The horses and their accoutrements were polished up to perfection, and he himself, in his dark-grey clothes and hard black hat, looked a model of discretion and neatness. The only one who lacked confidence was myself.

Stuffing a packet of sandwiches into my pocket and pulling on my uncomfortably new gloves, I felt half aware of certain shortcomings in my outward appearance. Ought one really to go out hunting in a brown corduroy suit with a corduroy jockey-cap to match the suit? Did other boys wear that sort of thing? . . . I was conscious, too, that Dixon was regarding me with an unusually critical eye. Mute and flustered, I mounted. Sheila seemed very fresh, and the saddle felt cold and slippery. As we trotted briskly through the village everything had an austerely unfamiliar look about it, and my replies to Dixon were clumsy and constrained. . . .

As we neared the meet I became more and more nervous. Not many of the hunting people came from our side of the country, and we saw no other horsemen to distract my attention until we rounded a bend of the road, and there at last was Finchurst Green, with the hounds clustering in a corner and men in red coats and black coats moving to and fro to keep their horses from getting chilled. . . . I will not invent

details which I cannot remember, since I was too awed and excited and self-conscious to be capable of observing anything clearly.

Once we had arrived, Dixon seemed to become a different Dixon, so dignified and aloof that I scarcely dared to speak to him. Of course I knew what it meant: I was now his young gentleman' and he was only the groom who had brought me to 'have a look at the hounds'. But there was no one at the meet who knew me, so I sat there, shy and silent—aware of being a newcomer in a strange world which I did not understand. Also I was quite sure that I should make a fool of myself. Other people have felt the same, but this fact would have been no consolation to me at the time, even if I could have realized it.

My first period of suspense ended when with much bobbing up and down of hats the cavalcade moved off along the road. I looked round for Dixon, but he allowed me to be carried on with the procession; he kept close behind me, however. He had been sensible enough to refrain from confusing me with advice before we started, and I can see now that his demeanour continued to be full of intuitive tactfulness. But he was talking to another groom, and I felt that I was being scrutinized and discussed.

I was riding alongside a large, lolloping lady in a blue habit; she did not speak to me; she confined herself to a series of expostulatory remarks to her horse, which seemed too lively and went bouncing along

sideways with its ears back, several times bumping into Sheila, whose behaviour was sedately alert.

Soon we turned in at some lodge gates, crossed the corner of an undulating park, and then everyone pulled up outside a belt of brown woodland. The hounds had disappeared, but I could hear the huntsman's voice a little way off. He was making noises which I identified as not altogether unlike those I had read about in Surtees. After a time the chattering crowd of riders moved slowly into the wood, which appeared to be a large one.

My first reaction to the "field" was one of mute astonishment. I had taken it for granted that there would be people "in pink," but these enormous confident strangers overwhelmed my mind with the visible authenticity of their brick-red coats. It all felt quite different to reading Surtees by the schoolroom fire.

But I was too shy to stare about me, and every moment I was expecting an outburst of mad excitement in which I should find myself galloping wildy out of the wood. When the outbreak of activity came I had no time to think about it. For no apparent reason the people around me (we were moving slowly along a narrow path in the wood) suddenly set off at a gallop and for several minutes I was aware of nothing but the breathless fury of being carried along, plentifully spattered with mud by the sportsman in front of me. Suddenly, without any warning, he pulled up. Sheila automatically followed suit, shooting me well up her neck. The next moment everyone turned round and we all went tearing back the way we had come. I found Dixon in front of me, and he turned his head with a grin of encouragement.

Soon afterwards the hunt came to a standstill in an open space in the middle of the wood; the excitement seemed to be abating, and I felt that fox-hunting wasn't so difficult as I'd expected it to be. . . .

The comparatively mild activities of the morning had occupied a couple of hours. We now trotted away from Major Gamble's preserves. It was about three miles to Hoath Wood; on the way several small spinneys were drawn blank, but Hoath Wood was a sure find, so Dixon said, and a rare place to get a gallop from. This caused a perceptible evaporation of the courage which I had been accumulating, and when there was a halt for the hunt-servants to change on to their second horses I made an attempt to dispel my qualms by pulling out my packets of sandwiches.

While I was munching away at these I noticed for the first time another boy of about my age. Dixon was watching him approvingly. Evidently this was a boy to be imitated, and my own unsophisticated eyes already told me that. He was near enough to us for me to be able to observe him minutely. A little aloof from the large riders round him, he sat easily, but very upright, on a corky chestnut pony with a trimmed stump of a tail and a neatly "hogged" neck.

Reconstructing that far-off mo-

ment, my memory fixes him in a characteristic attitude. Leaning slightly forward from the waist, he straightens his left leg and scrutinizes it with an air of critical abstraction. He seems to be satisfied with his smart buff breeches and natty brown gaiters. Everything he has on is neat and compact. He carries a small crop with a bark leather thong, which he flicks at a tuft of dead grass in a masterly manner. An air of self-possessed efficiency begins with his brown bowler hat, continues in his neatly tied white stock, and gets its finishing touch in the short, blunt, shining spurs on his black walking boots. (I was greatly impressed by the fact that he worse spurs.) All his movements were controlled and modest, but there was a suggestion of arrogance in the steady, unrecognizing stare which he gave me when he became conscious that I was looking at him so intently. Our eyes met, and his calm scrutiny reminded me of my own deficiencies in dress. I shifted uneasily in my saddle, and the clumsy unpresentable old hunting-crop fell out of my hand. Dismounting awkwardly to pick it up, I wished that it, also, had a thong (though this would make the double reins more difficult to manage) and I hated my silly jockey cap and the badly fitting gaiters which pinched my legs and always refused to remain in the correct position (indicated by Dixon). When I scrambled up on to Sheila again— a feat which I could only just accomplish without assistance—I felt what a poor figure I must be cutting in Dixon's eyes while he compared

me with that other boy, who had turned himself away with a slight smile and was now soberly following the dappled clustering pack and its attendant red-coats as they disappeared over the green, rising ground on their way to Hoath Wood.

By all the laws of aunthood we should by now have been well on our way home. But Dixon was making a real day of it. The afternoon hunt was going to be a serious affair. There never appeared to be any doubt about that. The field was reduced to about forty riders, and the chattersome contingent seemed to have gone home. We all went into the covert and remained close together at one end. Dixon got off and tightened my girths, which had got very loose (as I ought to have noticed). A resolute-looking lady in a tall hat drew her veil down after taking a good pull at the flask which she handed back to her groom. Hard-faced men rammed their hats on to their heads and sat silently in the saddle as though, for

235

the first time in the day, they really meant business. My heart was in my mouth and it had good reason to be there. Lord Dumborough was keeping an intent eye on the ride which ran through the middle of the covert.

"Cut along to the top end, Charlie," he remarked without turning his head; and a gaunt, ginger-haired man in a weather-stained scarlet coat went off up the covert in a squelchy canter.

"That's Mr. Macdoggart," said Dixon in a low voice, and my solemnity increased as the legendary figure vanished on its mysterious errand.

Meanwhile the huntsman was continuing his intermittent yaups as he moved along the other side of the wood. Suddenly his cheers of encouragement changed to a series of excited shoutings. "Hoick-holler, hoick-holler, hoick-holler!" he yelled, and then blew his horn loudly; this was followed by an outbreak of vociferation from the hounds, and soon they were in full cry across the covert. I sat there petrified by my private feelings; Sheila showed no symptoms of agitation; she merely cocked her ears well forward and listened.

And then, for the first time, I heard a sound which has thrilled generations of fox-hunters to their marrow. From the far side of the wood came the long shrill screech (for which it is impossible to find an adequate word) which signified that one of the whips has viewed the fox quitting the covert. "Gone away" it meant. But before I had formulated the haziest notion about

it, Lord Dumborough was galloping up the ride and the rest of them were pelting after him as though nothing could stop them. As I happened to be standing well inside the wood and Sheila took the affair into her own control, I was swept along with them, and we emerged on the other side among the leaders.

I cannot claim that I felt either excitement or resolution as we bundled down a long slope of meadow-land and dashed helter-skelter through an open gate at the bottom. I knew nothing at all except that I was out of breath and that the air was rushing to meet me, but as I hung onto the reins I was aware that Mr. Macdoggart was immediately in front of me. My attitude was an acquiescent one. I have always been inclined to accept life in the form in which it has imposed itself upon me, and on that particular occasion, no doubt, I just felt that I was "in for it". It did not so much as occur to me that in following Mr. Macdoggart I was setting myself rather a high standard, and when he disappeared over a hedge I took it for granted that I must do the same. For a moment Sheila hesitated in her stride. (Dixon told me afterwards that I actually hit her as we approached the fence, but I couldn't remember having done so.) Then she collected herself and jumped the fence with a peculiar arching of her back. There was a considerable drop on the other side. Sheila had made no mistake, but as she landed I left the saddle and flew over her head. I had let go of the reins, but she stood stock-still while I sat on the wet ground. A few mo-

ments later Dixon popped over a gap lower down the fence and came to my assistance, and I saw the boy on the chestnut pony come after him in a resolute but unhurrying way. I scrambled to my feet, feeling utterly ashamed.

"Whatever made you go for it like that?" asked Dixon, who was quite disconcerted.

"I saw Mr. Macdoggart going over it, and I didn't like to stop," I stammered. By now the whole hunt had disappeared and there wasn't a sound to be heard.

"Well, I suppose we may as well go on." He laughed as he gave me a leg up. "Fancy you following Mr. Macdoggart over the biggest place in the fence. Good thing Miss Sherston couldn't see you."

The idea of my aunt seemed to amuse him, as he slapped his knee and chuckled as he led me onward at a deliberate pace.

From "Henry the Fifth," by Shakespeare. An exchange among the Constable of France, Lord Rambures, the Duke of Orleans, and the Dauphin on the eve of the Battle of Agincourt, in 1415.

CONSTABLE: Tut! I have the best armor of the world. Would it were day!
ORLEANS: You have excellent armor, but let my horse have his due.
CONSTABLE: It is the best horse of Europe.
ORLEANS: Will it never be morning?
DAUPHIN: My Lord of Orleans, and my lord High Constable, you talk of horse and armor?

ORLEANS: You are as well provided of both as any prince in the world.

DAUPHIN: What a long night is this! I will not change my horse with any that treads but on four pasterns. *Ça, ha!* He bounds from the earth, as if his entrails were hairs; *le cheval volant*, the Pegasus, *chez les narines de feu!* When I bestride him, I soar, I am a hawk. He trots the air, the earth sings when he touches it, the barest horn of his hoof is more musical than the pipe of Hermes.

ORLEANS: He's the colour of the nutmeg.

DAUPHIN: And of the heat of the ginger. It is a beast for Perseus. He is pure air and fire, and the dull elements of earth and water never appear in him, but only in patient stillness while his rider mounts him. He is indeed a horse, and all other jades you may call beasts.

CONSTABLE: Indeed, my lord, it is a most absolute and excellent horse.

DAUPHIN: It is the prince of palfreys. His neigh is like the bidding of a monarch, and his countenance enforces homage.

ORLEANS: No more, cousin.

DAUPHIN: Nay, the man hath no wit that cannot, from the rising of the lark to the lodging of the lamb, vary deserved praise on my palfrey. It is a theme as fluent as the sea. Turn the sands into eloquent tongues and my horse is argument for them all. 'Tis a subject for a sovereign to reason on, and for a sovereign's sovereign to ride on, and for the world, familiar to us and unknown, to lay apart their particular functions and wonder at him. I once writ a sonnet in his praise, and began thus: "Wonder of nature—"

ORLEANS: I have heard a sonnet begin so to one's mistress.

DAUPHIN: Then did they imitate that which I composed to my courser, for my horse is my mistress.

ORLEANS: Your mistress bears well.

DAUPHIN: Me well, which is the prescript praise and perfection of a good and particular mistress.

CONSTABLE: Nay, for methought yesterday your mistress shrewdly shook your back.

DAUPHIN: So perhaps did yours.

CONSTABLE: Mine was not bridled.

DAUPHIN: O, then belike she was old and gentle, and you rode like a kern of Ireland, your French hose off and in your strait strossers.

CONSTABLE: You have good judgement in horsemanship.

DAUPHIN: Be warned by me, then. They that ride so and ride not warily fall into foul bogs. I had rather have my horse to my mistress.

CONSTABLE: I had as lief have my mistress a jade.

DAUPHIN: I tell thee, Constable, my mistress wears his own hair.

CONSTABLE: I could make as true a boast as that if I had a sow to my mistress.

DAUPHIN: *"Le chien est retourné à son propre vomissement, et la truie lavée au bourbier."* Thou makest use of anything.

CONSTABLE: Yet do I not use my horse for my mistress, or any such proverb so little kin to the purpose.

RAMBURES: My Lord Constable, the armor that I saw in your tent tonight, are those stars or suns upon it?

CONSTABLE: Stars, my lord.

DAUPHIN: Some of them will fall tomorrow, I hope.

CONSTABLE: And yet my sky shall not want.

DAUPHIN: That may be, for you bear a many superfluously, and 'twere more honor some were away.

CONSTABLE: Even as your horse bears your praises, who would trot as well were some of your brags dismounted.

DAUPHIN: Would I were able to load him with his desert! Will it never be day? I will trot tomorrow a mile, and my way shall be paved with English faces.

From "Mindy Lindy May Surprise," by Michael Erlanger.[3] This chapter of the novel describes Quarter horse racing as an aspect of larceny. The author vouches for the accuracy of the spirit of the extract.

"This place out in Nevada," said Archie, "is called Hunker Downs."

Dino never saw a sign that called it anything else. It was a flat place in the middle of some hills where a bulldozer had leveled out a strip of about a quarter of a mile or so. There was a snow fence painted white down one side of this. There were no stands but up on the side of the hill, by what Dino guessed was the finish line, somebody had put a few boards across some cement blocks for the women and children and the old and the infirm.

The secretary's office was an old army-surplus tin hut with the back half open for a counter where soda and franks were sold to the highest bidder. There was also an old five-stall starting gate up at the head of the strip, and this was operated from an extension cord plugged in through the window into the hut. It took five hours' driving time to get there.

"Well," said Archie, after they'd pulled up and parked. "There she is, Hunker Downs, the mecca of the last gasp. How you like it?"

"It's where elephants come to die," said Dino.

"Yeah," said Archie, "but they run them first. Old elephants three and up to go a mile and I'll give you five to three on the one with the trunk."

There were perhaps three hundred people milling around and forty or fifty horse trailers. Over by the stands some families were having picnics made up of soda and franks and mustard.

There were kids all over the place and women in slacks with their hair in steel. The men were mostly in a bunch over at the hut and around the trailers with the horses. Here and there were kids up on their ponies, and on the track two horses were being loaded into the starting gate.

Dino and Archie sat in the car and watched. The bell rang and the gate opened and one horse came out running. The other hit the track head-down and bellowing and bucking just like the Fourth of July in the movies. The kid riding it went ass over teakettle and the pony bucked on down the track. Everybody was cheering and waving and having a fine time. A boy on a palomino pony caught up the bronc and brought it back to the gate. This time when the bell rang, it was clear the pony had just been kidding around the time before. The boy on its back lasted one and a half jumps before saying goodbye, and then the pony really put on an exhibition till the saddle slipped under him, and he spooked and went hell for lightning down the track.

"Twenty-two and an eighth," said Archie. He had his watch out. "Near as I can figure four-forty."

"Nobody on its back," said Dino.

"It's still kiting," said Archie.

After they caught the pony they stripped off the racing saddle and put on a heavy western rig. A man came out buckling on his chaps, hitched them into place, pulled down his hat, and climbed on. They loaded the pony into the gate again, and this time when the bell rang both man and beast came out serious. The whole thing was too much for the little bronc, who wasn't more than three years old, and he stopped bucking after about fifteen jumps and stood spraddle-legged, nostrils cracking and blowing, his eyes white, and trembling in every limb. The man reached out and slapped him alongside the head with his hat, and the pony ducked and gave a half-hearted buck, but his heart wasn't in it any more. The man climbed off, and the kid who'd been riding him pulled off the heavy rig and led the pony away.

The pony gone, Archie's car got the attention. It was a big, old, oversized purple Caddy that belonged to his girl. It had a trailer hitch on behind and the back seat had been removed so they could haul the tack there.

Dino smoothed the orange jacket and turned to Archie. "Well," he said, "Shall we let them take us?"

"Ready on the right," said Archie.

It was very dusty, and Dino's cordovans were full of sand before he'd gone three steps. They walked over to the tin hut and went in. There were a bunch of men sitting around the room chewing straws and talking in one-word sentences. One long old boy sat behind a table.

"Mornin', boys," he said, speaking around the straw. "Interested in runnin' anythin'? You name it, we'll match it."

"We just come to look," said Archie. "Maybe pick up a horse worth the money. My friend here" —he pointed to Dino—"wants to buy a pony for his kids you hear of any around."

"Well," said the old boy behind

the table, "we got us a appaloosa race today. They make good kids' ponies. Stick around. Lookin's free."

"Thank you, sir," said Dino, and they wandered out.

Archie headed for the mustard shop, but Dino went toward the trailers to see if he could get a glimpse of Oil Dust and Hochmeister [a horse and its shady owner he and Archie had encountered earlier]. He stood there looking around him when he heard a snort, and turning, saw the little bronc that had put on the show out of the gate tied to the side of a trailer. Its ears were cocked and he was giving Dino the once-over. Nobody had bothered to cool him out, just tied him there still sweating and breathing hard. Dino stood quietly and looked. It was a nice chunky little bay horse built like a block of wood, with four short legs and a strong hind end. He had a smart wide head, deep-jawed and narrow-muzzled, and little ears with the tips pointing at each other. Dino began to talk to it and walked up slow, his hand outstretched. The pony backed up to the end of the rope and waited, his whole being centered on Dino. He let Dino touch him and slowly peel back his upper lip. The pony was no more than three at the most. He reminded Dino of Mindy back before the war. There were no swellings or bumps on the short black legs, but Dino wanted to feel them to see if they were cool. He ran his hand down the pony's shoulder, and suddenly the skin quivered and he heard a snort, and at the same time

a hind leg made a lethal reach at him. Dino ducked out and saw the pony wasn't looking at him but at a man behind him. It was the one who had ridden in the western saddle, a small wiry man with a nose and a jaw like a rusty razor.

"Make a nice kid's pony," he said to Dino. "My little girl rides him all over the ranch. Follows her like a dog."

"I like its color," said Dino. "Sort of a mahogany beige."

"Yep," said the man.

"But I wouldn't want one too young," said Dino. "My kid doesn't ride too good and I don't want to take a chance with a pony doesn't know anything."

"That pony's eight years old," said the man, "and he never made a bad move yet."

Dino decided it was his clothes. He remembered he had bought a handkerchief, so he took it out and wiped his hands and flicked the dust off the cordovans. "It certainly is dusty," he said.

"Yep," said the man. "That there's a real quarter bred horse. His daddy's Old Prong Tree Joe and his mammy's a mare I got down in Texico. A real good bred mare could scat in twenty-three [seconds] any time. I got papers you want to see them."

He reached into his pocket and handed Dino a piece of paper. It was a registration certificate for a quarter horse, a bay colt by the name of Joseph J, by Prong Tree Joe out of Yellow Maud. The markings were the same as on the little horse, a small diamond star and one hind leg white to the top of the fet-

lock. Dino figured the man thought he was too dumb to read, as the certificate was for a colt three years old and not eight as he had said. Dino passed over this.

"I'll take an even thousand for him," said the man.

"That's more than I figured to pay for a kid's pony," said Dino.

"It's high," said the man, "but I can see you like the best, and when it comes to kids the best is none too good. That's what I always say. I'll throw in a halter and shank."

"Knock it in half," said Dino, "and I'll take your word for it."

He took out his wallet and counted out five hundred dollars. He gave it to the man and watched him sign the certificate over to him. The man's name was Clint Benz, and it took him quite a while to figure how the letters went.

"Isn't that the same colt gave the boy such a fit out the gate?" said Dino.

"That's his twin brother," said the man. "I wouldn't give no pony

239

like that to a kid."

Dino looked at him, and the man spat on the ground and covered it with dust using his boot.

"Let me know can I help you get him home," he said. "I got a friend can sell you a trailer real cheap."

"I'll yell," said Dino.

"You do that," said the man.

Dino went to look for Archie. As he passed by a large blue trailer, he heard war declared inside it and this mad man's voice say, "You dumb broad. If you wasn't so old I'd break you apart." Then he heard somebody hit something, and then a horse banged the side of the trailer and snorted. Then he heard the dumb broad's voice, really steely, whiny but steely. "You put your husky hands on me again," it said, "and you won't never put anything in or on or around anybody again."

The side of the trailer banged again, and Hochmeister came out the door, and every vein in his face was cherry-red. Right behind him was the dumb broad. She was an overweight blonde in tight blue slacks and a bra, her hair a platinum platform around her head. Her eyes were black with mascara, but one of them was blacker and beginning to swell.

"How'd I know?" she yelled at Hochmeister. "I do human hair. How'd I know what color it would turn on a goddam horse."

She had a brush in her hand and she let it fly. It caught Hochmeister on the ear, and he turned and headed back up the ramp. She screamed and grabbed a pitchfork.

"You do," she said, pointing it at him, "and you'll be so full of holes you'll leak piss all over."

That stopped him. He looked at her and rubbed his ear where the brush had caught him.

"Okay," he said. Then he smiled. "But you got to admit I got the right to be mad."

She wasn't sure the war was over, and she hated to put down the pitchfork. He waited, and when she did, he passed her on the ramp and gave her a clout over the ear as she went by. She yelled, but the pitchfork was out of reach.

"Now we're even."

"Bastard," she said, but the war was over, and she knew it. She went to the front of the car and took out a pink sweater, which she pulled on over her hairdo. Then she looked in the side-view mirror, patted her hair, and took a close look at her eye. She reached in the front seat and brought out a make-up bag and went to work.

Hochmeister came back down the ramp leading the brown colt, and when he got out, Dino could see why he had been so mad. The whole rear end of the colt was covered with rosy spots like measles only bigger. Whatever she'd put on the colt hadn't worked the way it should. Peroxide, Dino decided. His sister Clara had tried once to be a blond and ended up rosy red after using it. Hochmeister saw him standing there.

"And she's a graduated beauty technician," he said. "It took three months and three hundred dollars to make her one and I paid every damn bit of it and this is what I

get. I'd sure hate like hell to see what she'd of done to this poor little horse before she learned how."

"Will you scratch him?" said Dino.

"For why?" said Hochmeister. "He's got spots, ain't he?"

"Yeah," said Dino, "and he doesn't itch."

He went to find Archie, who'd dug up something to spike the mustard with, so they had some and a soda and watched the heats.

"I bought me a kid's pony," said Dino. "The one you said went in twenty-three."

"Good," said Archie. "Who's the kid?"

"Me," said Dino.

The heats weren't much. There were four or five lightweight kids who could hang on a horse and an old wrinkled guy who was so drunk he couldn't. They ran off three or four horses at a time. The races were made up haphazardly, one owner challenging another and a purse of ten or twenty dollars being put up with a blanket thrown in. With maybe two more horses added, the bets were made, and somebody given the stakes to hold. Benz was right in the middle of it all, and Dino spotted him booking bets. It all seemed good-natured.

When the big race, the lollapaloosa one, came up, Dino went over to where Benz was standing.

"Can I bet on this race?" he said.

"How much you want to bet?" said Benz. "And on which horse?"

"The merry-go-round horse, there," said Dino, pointing to Hochmeister and Oil Dust. "A hundred dollars."

"That's Warpaint," said Benz. "Make it five."

"I only bet that much once," said Dino, "and that was in Las Vegas shooting crap."

"Pay for the kid's pony," said Benz.

"Might as well be hung for a goose as a gander," said Dino and counted it out.

They were leading the hometown flash down toward the gate, and it was obvious he'd been shot with a whole chain of drugstores. He was white-eyed and sweating and five feet off the ground. A heavy old man in jeans was hanging onto his head, trying to keep him going in the right direction. Right in back of him was Hochmeister and his merry-go-round horse, and the little brown colt was as full of dope as the hometown wonder. Dino watched him trying to get loose, and his anger juices stirred. Oil Dust was too nice a little horse to get screwed up this way. Once on the needle it was too hard to get them to put out without it.

"The hell with him," said Dino.

The third horse in the race was a lazy old yellow and white mare with a kid on it, and it had to be his first race just by the happy look on his face.

"Two hopheads and a stiff," said Archie. "What a larceny."

They loaded the three into the gate, the bell rang, out they came, and it was the kid on the yellow and white horse all the way. Oil Dust was second, beating the lollapaloosa by a length and a half.

The two were so hopped it took a mile to stop them.

"Which one is Benz?" said Archie.

"The one with the black face," said Dino.

"They're all black," said Archie.

The only happy space on Hunker Downs was where the kid's rooters stood, and they shone like a rainbow on a rainy day. The yellow horse jogged up to them, and Dino caught a glimpse of the kid's smiling face, and he remembered the day he had stolen his first on Mindy Lindy. Me and Eddie Lang, he thought, and kissed his five hundred goodbye.

After a while he looked up Benz and bought his friend's trailer, an old beat-up homemade job. Then he and Archie took off their good jackets and spent a warm fifteen minutes convincing Joseph J to get in it. They started off, and the trailer held together.

Outside of Sacramento, Archie turned to Dino. "What they call that yellow horse?" he said.

"Yellow Fever," said Dino.

"The hell," said Archie. "That's an old race mare name of Flaming Mamie. I wouldn't of missed her only I didn't watch her move before the race. I claimed her once over a year ago and only got to run her once before they took her back. She could scat in twenty-three any time on a hard track. She can't run for peanuts in the slop."

He was quiet for a mile or so.

"That was some dye job," he said. "Almost as good as Hochmeister's. I wonder what color the hometown lollapaloosa is."

[1] Reprinted by permission of Longman Group, Ltd.
[2] Reprinted by permission of Faber and Faber, Ltd. from *Memoirs of a Fox-Hunting Man*; reprinted by permission of Stackpole Books, from *Memoirs of a Fox-Hunting Man*, by Siegfried Sassoon.
[3] By permission of Michael Erlanger, © 1969.

Index

Acknowledgments

The author and publishers wish to express their deep appreciation of the generous assistance of the following organizations and individuals in the preparation of this book.

Albright-Knox Art Gallery, Buffalo; American Museum of Natural History, New York; Amon Carter Museum, Fort Worth; Amtskasse der Bayerischen Staatsgemäldesammlungen, Munich; Archaeological Museum, Valencia; Archives de France; Ashmolean Museum, Oxford University; Bibliothèque Nationale, Paris; Bodleian Library, Oxford University; British Museum, London; Brooklyn Museum, New York; Budd Studios, New York; City Art Museum, St. Louis; Cleveland Museum of Art, Holden Collection, Cleveland; Cliché des Musées Nationaux, France; Collection Alice Boney, New York; Collection of the Marquess of Bath, England; Columbus Gallery of Fine Arts, Columbus, Ohio; Courtauld Institute of Art, London; Conzett & Huber, Zurich; Culver Pictures, New York; Danish National Museum, Copenhagen; Denver Art Museum, Denver; Fitzwilliam Museum, Cambridge University; Fogg Art Museum, Cambridge; Freer Gallery of Art, Washington, D.C.; Frick Art Reference Library, New York; Galerie Charpentier, Paris; Goethe Museum, Frankfurt am Main; Imperial Science Museum, London; Knoedler Galleries, New York; Kozan-ji, Kyoto; Patrick Lynch, Gladstone, New York; Metropolitan Museum of Art, New York; Musée Bonnat, Bayonne; Musée du Petit-Palais, Paris; Museo Profano Lateranense, Rome; Museum of Fine Arts, Boston; National Army Museum, London; National Gallery, London; National Gallery, Oslo; National Gallery of Art, Washington, D.C.; National Gallery of Ireland, Dublin; New York Public Library, New York; New York State Historical Association, Cooperstown; Walter Osborne, California; Pierpont Morgan Library, New York; Philbrook Art Center, Tulsa; Pierpont Morgan Library, New York; Royal Library, Windsor; Smithsonian Institution, Washington, D.C.; Tate Gallery, London; United Press International; Victoria and Albert Museum, London; Walker Art Gallery, Liverpool; Wallace Collection, London; Walters Art Gallery, Baltimore; West Point Museum Collection, West Point; Wide World Photos, New York.

The Life, History and Magic of the Horse
was prepared and produced by Chanticleer Press:
Publisher: Paul Steiner
Editor: Milton Rugoff. Associate: Marjorie Rutimann, Celeste Marder
Art Director: Ulrich Ruchti. Associate: Irva Mandelbaum
Production Manager: Gudrun Buettner. Associate: Emma Staffelbach
Printed by Dai Nippon Printing Co., Ltd., Tokyo, Japan